"Missional": Embracing a Paradigm Shift for Missions

Papers presented at the Conference
of the Association of Evangelical Missiology (AfeM)
in Cooperation with Mission-Net Congress 2013/14

edition afem
mission reports 22

afem

Robert Badenberg
Friedemann Knödler
(Eds.)

VTR
Publications

This book ist part of the series edition afem,
ed. by Thomas Schirrmacher, Bernd Brandl,
Friedemann Knödler, and Thomas Mayer.
http://www.missiologie.org

Bibliographic information published by the Deutsche Nationalbibliothek
The Deutsche Nationalbibliothek lists this publication in the Deutsche National-
bibliografie; detailed bibliographic data are available in the Internet at
http://dnb.d-nb.de.

ISBN 978-3-95776-014-2
ISSN 0944-6133

© 2015

2nd amended edition

VTR Publications
Gogolstr. 33, 90475 Nürnberg, Germany
http://www.vtr-online.com

Cover Illustration: VTR Publications
Layout: Friedemann Knödler

Contents

Foreword

Robert Badenberg[1]

Have we not had enough controversial topics in recent years? Cape Town 2010 vis-à-vis Edinburgh 2010 seemingly upholding the dichotomy between evangelism and social responsibility; the emergent church movement swapping over from North America causing a stir in the evangelical arena across Europe; the heated debate on the theology of transformation – just to name a few. And to add yet another topic loaded with ideas, approaches, and theological convictions: 'missional'. Though not an entirely new missiological theme, thanks to Lesslie Newbigin's discourse with Western culture starting in the 1980s, it impacts contemporary mission thought and practice on a fundamental level. Are we then just jumping on the latest bandwagon and enjoying a ride while it lasts?

As Association of evangelical Missiology (AfeM), we wish to be apprehensive of current issues. No, we do not just jump on the latest bandwagon enjoying a ride while it lasts. We see it our duty to not shy away from issues, even controversial ones. We seek to participate in the discussion but as one who invites the participants and sits them around a table in order to have an informative discussion. "Eye to eye" – as it were.

The compilation of this edition of the yearbook follows the tradition of all previously published editions of yearbooks in as much as it contains the presentations of the speakers delivered at the Annual Meeting of AfeM. New, however, is the context within which the presentations were delivered. Instead of staging our traditional conference for our members and other missiological clientele, AfeM co-operated with Mission-Net when they hosted their third conference in Offenburg, Germany, from December 28, 2013 to January 2, 2014.

Naturally, this set up was not without challenges and there were obvious drawbacks, for instance, the "rather little interaction possible between 'classical AfeM-members and Mission-Net players'", as one voice stated it. And on a positive note, there where young people who appreciated AfeM's presence by offering theological, cultural and societal aspects of 'being missional' through keynote lectures. Nevertheless, we tried something new and we exercised networking. Just to make a point here: It so happened that the Taizé Community had organized their annual European Young Adults Meeting in Strasbourg and in the surrounding places in Alsace and in the Ortenau. Because of this constellation, it was arranged – and possible – to have Frère Richard come to Offenburg and give a lecture on the missional life of the Taizé Community.

The reader will find that the arrangement of the articles in this volume follows the program of the meeting in its theoretical outline as well as in the sequence of lec-

---

[1] Robert Badenberg, DTh, teaches at Akademie für Weltmission, Korntal; Wycliff Centre Germany, etp program; visiting professor of missiology at Theological Faculty «Matija Vlačić Ilirik», Zagreb; Secretary of the Association of Evangelical Missiology (AfeM).

tures as they were delivered. The article by Thomas Schirrmacher, however, is not part of the original presentations of the conference but a suitable add-on for this edition.

One will easily note that the presentations on 'missional practice' outweigh the lectures on the 'why' and 'which' questions of doing missions. This volume benefits from a wide range of cultural contexts and church settings spanning from Portugal to Latvia and from Moldova to the United Kingdom. The contributions made by missiologists from Latvia and Moldova are especially noteworthy as they introduce us to mission contexts, which are rather sparingly represented within missiological literature.

The reader will also find that we have diverted from the usual language of publication, German, and opted for English. The reason is twofold: First, all the presentations were given in that language and second, a wider distribution of this volume is possible.

We hope to make a valuable contribution to the 'missional' discussion by presenting this volume to our traditional readership – and to those beyond! – and wish for it to achieve a wide circle of distribution. Moreover, we hope to stir some hearts for re-evangelizing Europe and invite you to pray with us the simple prayer:

God bless Europe!

Johannes Reimer[1]

Which Views of Mission Help Us in Our Contemporary Situation?

The World We Live in

Mission in heterogeneous contexts – the topic of our first seminar indicates a context consisting of parts which traditionally may not belong together; they may be cultural, social, political or religious.[2] The heterogeneous world is a patchwork of culture, is multioptional and pluriform in principle. P. Cross calls such a world a "multioptional society".[3] This is a world full of challenge and risk.[4]

There are many places in the world which may claim a similar condition. Europe, for instance, has *en large* become such a world. European societies and cultures are in transition from a mono- to a heterogeneous format. And this means, as Lothar Käser rightly points out, mission will go through a transition.[5] You simply cannot do mission as usual in cultural diverse contexts.[6] Some even suggest there is no place for mission in a pluralistic world.[7] Klaus Müller's Book title describes the situation we face well – "Mission in crossfire."[8] But how do we do missions in pluralistic societies? How do we stay faithful to God's calling and at the same time become successful in proclaiming the Gospel in a world of plurality? How do we think and how do we do mission in a world of diversity, with neighbours from different continents and of different cultural and religious convictions? What approaches to missions are still relevant?

---

[1] Johannes Reimer, DTh, Professor of Missiology at the Theologische Hochschule Ewersbach (Germany) and the University of South Africa, Department of Christian Spirituality, Church History and Missiology. Chairman of Gesellschaft für Bildung und Forschung in Europa (GBFE).

[2] Richard D. Lewis offers an excellent introduction into what we call heterogeneous contexts in his book: Richard D. Lewis. 2006. *When Cultures collide. Leading across Cultures.* Third edition. Boston/London: Nicolas Brealy International, pp.3-16.

[3] Peter Gross, 1994. *Multioptionsgesellschaft.* Fankfurt: Suhrkamp.

[4] The German sociologist Ulrich Beck uses the term "Risikogesellschaft" = "risk society" to underline the many currents influencing our "other modernity". See: Ulrich Beck. 1986. *Risikogesellschaft.* Frankfurt.

[5] Lothar Käser. 2001. Der positive und negative Beitrag der Mission zur gesellschaftlichen und kulturellen Entwicklung, in: Klaus W. Müller (Hg). *Mission im Kreuzfeuer.* Referate der Jahrestagung 2001 des Arbeitskreises für evangelikale Missiologie (AfeM). Edition afem/mission reports 9. Nürnberg: VTR, p.23.

[6] There are many well written books and articles on the importance of culture in communication of the gospel. See, for instance, David J. Hesselgrave. 1978. *Communicating Christ Cross-Culturally. An Introduction to missionary communication.* Grand Rapids: Zondervan, pp.67-120.

[7] See the discussion in Andreas Feldtkeller. 1999. Pluralismus – was nun? Eine missionstheologische Standortbestimmung. In: Andreas Feldtkeller, Theo Sundermeier (Hrsg). *Mission in pluralistischer Gesellschaft.* Frankfurt a.M.: Otto Lembeck Verlag, pp.42-47.

[8] Klaus W. Müller, *Mission im Kreuzfeuer.*

David J. Bosch in his opus magna, *Transforming mission,* suggested an upcoming ecumenical paradigm of mission in which he defined 13 elements.[9] Each of his characteristics suggests one or more mission approaches and methods of realization. Most of them can be easily applied to our topic as well. In view of limited time and space given for my presentation, I will concentrate on four of his characteristics, summing up the rest under these four: (1) mission as evangelism; (2) mission as church growth; (3) mission as transformation; (4) mission as community development.

To answer the question of my paper, I will (a) name the four mission views and approaches in praxis, (b) critically look at both their theological foundation and practical validity, and (c) name a possible matrix for developing a missional view and, possibly, a *Handlungstheorie* (theory of action) for missions in heterogeneous contexts.

Missions Vary – Results Prove

The four selected *mission theories of action* are typical approaches used in heterogeneous contexts of Europe by evangelicals today.

a. Evangelism centred approach. Representatives of this approach may be found in most of our evangelical denominations with a strong pietistic tradition. The world in their view is corrupted by sin and lost; cultures are totally deprived, and Christ appears as the ultimate alternative, clearly positioned against every culture. Richard Niebuhr (1894-1962) once called such an approach "Christ against Culture".[10] The evangelical exclusivist would see little difference between a mono- and a heterogeneous context. All culture is equally corrupted by sin and will be equally rejected by faithful Christians.[11] Their mission perspective is *salvation from the world,* and the only valid instrument of mission is *preaching* the Gospel of salvation.[12] Salvation is described as an inward change of the human heart condition, the freedom from sin and demonic dominance.[13] Surely enough, inwardly changed people will live a sanctified life, promote a different culture, but this culture is exclusively lived out in the church. Aggressive evangelism and church planting are at the heart of this mission approach.[14] Missional involvement in society is regarded as potentially syncretistic

---

[9] David J. Bosch. 1991. *Transforming mission: Paradigm shifts in mission theology.* Maryknoll: Orbis Books, pp.368-510.

[10] Richard Niebuhr. 1951. *Christ and Culture.* New York, NY: Harper &Row. pp.47-48.

[11] Charles H. Kraft. 1979. *Christianity in Culture. A Study in Dynamic Biblical Theologizing in Cross-Cultural Perspective.* Maryknoll: Orbis, pp.104-106.

[12] See the debate on the issue of Evangelism as the one and only content of mission from a perspective of Evangelical exclusivist position in: Arthur Johnson. 1978. *The Battle for World Evangelism.* Wheaton: Tyndale House; In German this book was published as *Umkämpfte Weltmission.*1984. Neuhausen-Stuttgart: Hänssler Verlag.

[13] See discussion in Walter Klaiber. 1990. *Ruf und Antwort. Biblische Grundlagen einer Theologie der Evangelisation.* Stuttgart: Christliches Verlagshaus, pp.191-192. A practical example: Anton Schulte. 1979. *Evangelisation praktisch. Mit Anmerkungen zu einer deutschen „Theologie der Evangelisation".* Moers: Brendow Verlag, pp.111-112.

[14] Donald A. McGavran. 1983, What is Mission? In: A.F. Glasser & D.A. McGavran (ed). *Contemporary Theologies of Mission.* Grand Rapids: Baker Book, p.17.

and is, therefore, discouraged. Any dialogue with the world, the living religions and ideologies is regarded as dangerous and corruptive.[15]

Though still widely used in many European settings, this approach has lost its momentum almost everywhere in Europe.[16] People seem to avoid Christian revival crusades, tent missions, etc. Even in Eastern Europe, where the global church has invested billions of Euros for evangelization of the atheist population in the 1990s, aggressive evangelism appears less and less successful.[17]

b. Church Growth centred approach. Western, including European, churches have been greatly influenced by the American Church Growth movement. This movement was initiated by Donald A. McGavran (1897-1990), an American missiologist from Pasadena, CA, and his students at Fuller Theological Seminary, so for instance C. Peter Wagner. McGavran was a third-generation missionary to India. In his fifty years of missionary career he became concerned about the low conversion rate in his mission agency, despite the large investment of personnel and finances. So he devoted himself to the study of the factors that lead to church growth. Upon returning to the USA, McGavran founded the School of World Mission at Fuller Theological Seminary in California. His books on principles of church growth and evangelism have been translated into many languages. The basic idea of the movement is found in the Homogenous Unit principle (HU), presented to a larger audience for the first time in his book *The Bridges of God: A Study in the Strategy of Missions,* published in 1954.[18] Donald McGavran says: "The homogeneous unit is simply a section of society in which all the members have some characteristics in common. Thus a homogeneous unit (or HU, as it is called in church growth jargon) might be a political unit or sub-unit, the characteristic in common being that all the members live within certain geographical confines."[19]

Concentrating missionary effort on such units will, according to McGavran's theory, result in conversions and, finally, church growth. According to McGavran, Homogeneous Unit is a principle.[20] Critical thinkers, however, pointed to the missing biblical and theological justification and foundation of the HU principle.[21] Despite such

---

[15] Peter Beyerhaus. 1987. *Krise und Neuaufbruch der Weltmission.* Bad Liebenzell: VLM, pp.83-110.

[16] See the introductory chapter in my book on Evangelism: Johannes Reimer. 2013. *Leben. Rufen. Verändern: Chancen und Herausforderungen gesellschaftstransformatorischer Evangelisation heute.* Marburg: Francke Buchhandlung.

[17] See for instance: Catherine Wanner, 2004. Missionaries of Faith and Culture: Evangelical Encounters in Ukraine. In; *Slavic Review* 63(4), 732-755; Catherine Wanner, 2009. Missionaries and Pluralism: How the Law Changed the Religious Landscape in Ukraine, in: Onyshkevych, Larissa and Maria G. Rewakowicz, (Hg.), Contemporary Ukraine on the Cultural Map *of Europe,* Armonk, NY: Ruvim Voloshin, Vozvedite ochi vashi i posmotrite na nivy kak oni pobeleli i pospeli k Zhatve, in: http://baptist.org.ru/articles/missions/ (1.02.2013).

[18] Donald A. McGavran. 1954. *The Bridges of God: A Study in the Strategy of Missions.* Pasadena: WCL.

[19] Donald A. McGavran.1980. *Understanding Church Growth.* Grand Rapids: Eerdmans, p.95.

[20] Ibid, 243.

[21] See, for instance: Wilbert R. Shenk. (Ed.) 1973. *Exploring Church Growth.* Grand Rapids: Eerdmans, p.22; George W. Peters. 1981. *A Theology of Church Growth.* Grand Rapids: Zondervan, p.229-230; Costas, Orlando E. 1982. *Christ Outside the Gate.* Maryknoll: Orbis, p.43f.

critique, the church growth movement became one of the major mission approaches in most of our European evangelical denominations in the years between 1980 and 2000.[22] Mission in this movement is defined as evangelism leading to church planting and church growth and is praised as the most effective tool of God's salvific mission in the world,[23] which aims towards salvation of the soul and is not interested in the matters of the world.[24]

Today, years after the first presentation of McGavran's principles, the evaluation of results proves many weaknesses of the approach.[25] The promised revival falls short, fostering instead "transfer growth" for some churches while emptying others, and at the same time concentrating mission of the church in the (social) middle class. Some authors even speak of the "suburban captivity of the church".[26] Large segments of a given context appear unevangelized because few active Christians among them are found, and the active ones are preoccupied with evangelizing their kind of people. The Church Growth approach proves to be just as strongly limited in reaching heterogeneous contexts. Thus, the principle of HU appears more like a hindrance for mission in a multicultural space.[27]

c. Transformation centred approach. In contrast to most mainstream evangelicals, Radical Evangelicals[28] view the mission task of the church less as *salvation from the world*. With Apostle Paul, they would rather speak of *salvation of the world*, quoting 2 Cor 5:18-20. Here the church is seen as an ambassador of reconciliation of the world with God. The gospel proclaimed is classified as the gospel of the kingdom (Mt 1:17) and mission as transformation of whole nations (Mt 28:19-20); while nations – *ta ethne* – are understood as socio-political space. In such concepts cultures are never completely rejected, but rather transformed wherever they are corrupted by evil forces. Richard Niebuhr classified such a correlation between Christ and culture as "Christ transforms culture".[29] Mission here is traditionally described in the three terms of Gisbertus Voetus – *marturia*, *diaconia* and *leiturgia*: witness, service and worship or proclamation.[30] The intent is clearly holistic. Cultures are not rejected, but rather accepted as God-given. Mission may transform, but never dissolve them. The theology derives its motivation from the practice of life in a certain context and, therefore, informs action; it is basically doing theology, transcending all strata of life.

---

[22] For the German context, see: Fritz and Christian Schwarz. 1984. *Theologie des Gemeindebaus. Ein Versuch*. Neukirchen-Vluyn: Aussaat; a.o.

[23] See the reflection on published sources in Johannes Reimer. 2013. *Die Welt umarmen. Theologie des gesellschaftsrelevanten Gemeindebaus*. Marburg: Francke, p.17f.

[24] Donald A. McGavran. 1973. Salvation today, in: Ralph Winter, ed. *Evangelical Response to Bangkok*. Pasadena: WCL, pp.27-32.

[25] See in this regard: Paul E. Engle and Gary L. McIntosh. (eds.) 2004. *Evaluating Church Growth*. Grand Rapids: Zondervan.

[26] Gibson Winter. 1961. *The suburban captivity of the churches*. Doubleday; S.C.M. Press.

[27] See more and in detail in Johannes Reimer. 2011. *Multikultureller Gemeindebau. Versöhnung leben*. Marburg: Francke, pp.156ff.

[28] For history and theology of mission among the radical evangelicals, see the excellent DTh dissertation of Roland Hardmeier. 2012. *Kirche ist Mission*. Schwarzenfeld: Neufeld Verlag.

[29] Niebuhr, *Christ and Culture*, p.196.

[30] See more in Reimer, *Die Welt umarmen*, pp.195-197.

Most of the modern days' transformational theology of mission builds on David J. Bosch's *Transforming mission*[31] and seeks to implement a holistic missional approach. Mission here is understood as proclamation of God's Kingdom in word and deed, and mission praxis includes all of God's activity in the world.[32] And the church involved in transformative mission is viewed as a missional church, as missionary by her very nature and in all she is and does.[33] Her mission follows God's mission.

Mission as transformation is culturally sensitive and at the same time interested in transforming cultures and in discipling them into a culture of the kingdom of God. Their main aim is to promote and foster life. Therefore Andreas Feldtkeller defines mission as "Weitergabe des Lebens = passing on of life".[34] Here the Christian church is close to the people and their daily struggle for a better life. In a multi-optional society you are always surrounded by multiple options to win your struggle. Dialogue becomes a way of life. Borrowing the better ideas from your neighbour is a normal act. Understanding the dynamics of a pluralistic society, the church will have to involve herself in a dialogue and action for better living. And living the better option, she becomes a living witness to the non-believing world around her. Theo Sundermeier suggested implying a tri-dimensional matrix of dialogue, the art of "living together" and developing appropriate approaches for missions in pluralistic societies.[35] A suggestion, I think, which may help to work on contextually relevant transformational mission ideas for a particular European context. So, clearly, here lies great potential for mission in heterogeneous contexts of Europe.

d. Community centred approach. Mission as God's holistic enterprise into the world, as defined by transformational missiology, is asking for a specific role of the church. David J. Bosch has prophetically pointed to the rise of the role of the local church as well as to the question of community in general in his critical reflections on the San Antonia Mission Conference in 1989. He writes: "...the search for community will turn out to be a major missiological theme during the 1990s."[36] In his view, "... it is the *community* that is the primary bearer of mission."[37] He especially pointed to Western culture with its growing individualism as the main field where he imagined that a community centred approach might become central to the mission of the church.[38] Others supported his prophetic vision by analysing the situation. McCoy, for instance, postulates, "... community *in its own right* as a new or emerging paradigm of mission for a postmodern world?"[39] In the Western world, commu-

---

[31] Bosch. *Transforming mission.*

[32] See articles in: Jamie A. Grant and Dewi A. Hughes. 2009. *Transforming the World? The Gospel and social responsibility.* Nottingham: IVP.

[33] Reimer, *Die Welt umarmen*, p.261ff.

[34] Feldtkeller, *Pluralismus*, p.29.

[35] Theo Sundermeier. 1999. Mission und Dialog in pluralistischer Gesellschaft, in: Feldtkeller/Sundermeier, *Mission in pluralistischer Gesellschaft*, pp.24-25.

[36] David J. Bosch. 1989. Your will be done? Critical reflections on San Antonio. *Missionalia* 17/2 (August 1989), p.13.

[37] Bosch. *Transforming mission*, p.472.

[38] David J. Bosch. 1995. *Believing in the future: Toward a missiology of western culture.* Valley Forge: Trinity Press International.

[39] Michael McCoy. "Community": A postmodern mission paradigm? A forum paper presented at the

nity centred mission seems to have captured the imagination. A whole range of recent publications has literally flooded the market since 2000.[40] Guder carefully
summarizes the basic idea of the approach: The church's calling is to live in the
world as an apostle of God's reign, being an alternative community whose "inner,
communal life ... matters for mission."[41] Rene Padilla, and with him many others,
calls the Local Church the agent of transformation.[42]

Community centred mission does not just imply mission for church planting, but,
rather, church planting becomes a central part of a holistic, integral change process
of the context, of its cultural, social and political structure. Mission works for a better life in all regards, a life ruled by God's salvific intention to transform a nation
into his disciple (Mt 28:19-20). Thus, mission becomes an agent of the art of "living
together",[43] opening space for every member of a given context to participate. The
church in such a concept is not just a "church for others", as Dietrich Bonhoeffer
puts it,[44] but a *church with others*,[45] never losing sight of its alternative sacred nature, but always aware of her incarnate body in the midst of the world.

Toward a Missional Matrix for Missions in Heterogeneous Contexts

All approaches of mission discussed in my paper are seemingly set out to define
mission by clarifying the following terms: mission, the world, aim of mission, agent
of mission.

For the first group, mission is basically the same as proclamation of evangelism,
aiming to call sinners to leave the "world" and gather in churches in expectation of a
new earth and a new heaven. Kingdom of God is understood futuristically. The present context is neglected. The approach is to be praised for its sincerity, but it does
obviously not respond to the specific needs and potential challenges of heterogeneous contexts.

Southern African Missiological Society congress, "Issues facing the local church in mission at the
beginning of the 21st century", University of Pretoria, 24 January 2001.

[40] See in this regard: George R. Hunsberger & Craig Van Gelder (eds). 1996. *The church between gospel and culture: The emerging mission in North America.* Grand Rapids: Eerdmans; Loren B. Mead.
1991. *The once and future church: Reinventing the congregation for a new mission frontier.* Washington DC: Alban Institute; Alan J. Roxburgh. 1997. *The missionary congregation, leadership &
liminality.* Harrisburg: Trinity Press International; Robert Warren. 1995. *Being human, being
church: Spirituality and mission in the local church.* London: Marshall Pickering; Johannes Reimer.
2013. *Die Welt umarmen. Theologie des gesellschaftsrelevanten Gemeindebaus.* Marburg: Francke;
a.o.

[41] Darrell L. Guder (ed). 1998. *Missional church: A vision for the sending of the church in North
America.* Grand Rapids: Eerdmans, 1998, p.128.

[42] Tetsunao Yamamori and C. Rene Padilla. 2004. *The Local Church, Agent of Transformation.* Bue-
nos Aires: Kairos, p.19ff; Bosch, *Transforming Mission*, p.378-379.

[43] Theo Sundermeier. 1995. *Konvivenz und Differenz: Studien zu einer verstehenden Missionswissen-
schaft,* Hg. Volker Küster. Erlangen.

[44] Bonhoeffer. *DBW* 8, p.560 f..

[45] Bosch, *Transforming Mission*, p.368ff.

Our second group is similarly minded, but stresses the church as a sacred place where the kingdom of God is partially realized. Context is taken seriously, but only in regard to the specific techniques of communicating the gospel. Those might be helpful in terms of specific evangelistic actions, but proves problematic as a total strategy of mission.

The third group defines mission as a process of transforming the whole world, which is invited to reconcile with God, implying a world partially separated from God, corrupted by sin und in need of change and salvation. The gospel is understood here as a gospel of the kingdom and evangelism is proclamation in life, deed and word. Mission is seen as holistic, aiming for salvation of all life and all culture.

This approach takes the context seriously as a whole, sees and values cultural differences, and aims for transformation in the light of God's kingdom.

And the fourth and last group stresses the church as an alternative community sent to change the social environment to a place of godly living. Similar to transformational mission, the community centred approach seeks to transcend all life through the gospel proclaimed by the church through life, deed and word. This approach is in many regards a copy of the previous one and carries all potential to transform multicultural settings.

We may now conclude: mission approaches, designed for mission in heterogeneous contexts and probably as well as any context, will have to clarify their theological foundation of what mission is, name the target and the condition of the target of mission, decide on the agent of mission, and name the proposed outcome. Where those terms stay unclarified, mission will stay preliminarily undone und problematic. The transformational and community centred model of mission bears good potential for missions in our European multifaceted societies.

Vladimir Ubeivolc[1]

Why Do We Struggle with Our Traditional Mission Concepts?

A Case Study from an Orthodox Context: Analytical and Synthetic Evaluation of the Missiological Paradigms

Being in a post-everything context, the contemporary Church tries to evaluate not only its practice, but also its theological affirmations, understanding that one flows from another and overflows to the next. Being in a post-modern, post-constructionist, post-communist, post-cold war era, post-Christendom, post-institutionalized church context, Christian theologians, missiologists and pastors are confused. Everybody talks about post-everything, and their voices sound very critical, sometimes very analytical, very often prophetical, but not always synthetic.

Being a missiologist, I should be analytical and critical, but being a pastor, I should be synthetic. My responsibility is not only evaluation of the actual situation, but also bringing forth suggestions. The main question for this presentation is: Why do we struggle with our traditional mission concepts? I think that there are many reasons for our struggle, and most of them are objective and real. I could construct my paper, using general words and providing reasons, which are well-known in missiological circles, such as lack of relevant theological foundation for a postmodern world; theological and practical conservatism and reactionism; fear of unknown methods and tools, etc. But I will concentrate on a few concrete points.

Steve Moore published a book in 2012 with the topic of '*Seize of Vuja De*: a fresh look at challenges and opportunities of North American missions'.[2] He writes: "*Vuja De* is the ability to look at something familiar like you have never seen it before ... We are blind to our own blindness. This is why it is so hard to break out of our entrenched patterns of thought and action and why *vuja de* is so important."[3] So, I suggest using *vuja de* as a concept for re-evaluating the Church's mission.

So, what is the Mission of the Church and why do we struggle with our traditional mission concept? How is it related to the Mission of God and what role does it have in the development of the *Missio Dei* concept? In fact, it can be stated with certainty that the mission of the Church is directly related to the mission of God. A. Fernando said: "Jesus makes a connection between the nature of the church and the nature of the Trinity, even describing the church as a mirror of the Trinity."[4] Thus, by reflect-

---

[1] Rev. Vladimir Ubeivolc, PhD in Contextual Missiology, Executive director at Beginning of Life (NGO) and pastor of Light to the World church (Moldova), Lecturer of Missiology at Divitia Gratiae University (Moldova).

[2] Missio Nexus.

[3] Ibid, 1.

[4] Ajith Fernando. 2000. 'The Church: the mirror of the Trinity', in Taylor, W.D. (ed.), *Global Missiology for the 21st Century: the Iguassu Dialogue*. (Grand Rapids, MI: Baker Academic), p.241.

ing God, the Church fulfils the mission of God; and in order to do this, the Church has to know what God is doing.

Misunderstanding of Our Own Context Causes Struggles in Adopting New Mission Concepts

I made a research in Eastern European Orthodox contexts, in such countries as Moldova, Romania, Ukraine, Bulgaria and Russia. My research was focused on different missiological paradigms, which are used by Evangelicals in Orthodox countries, and on the produced results. First we are going to look at the differences existing between Evangelical and Orthodox missiology. Then I will try to find the similarities between them, and, in the end, I will formulate a coherent, synthetic missiology of the Church as the Body of Christ located in a predominantly Orthodox country.

Orthodox Missiology Vis-a-vis the Church Growth Movement

The Church Growth Movement (CGM) was one of those movements launched in a country with liberal-democratic values – the USA. The freedoms of speech and religion have been highly appreciated there since the founding day of that country. The United States are populated by immigrants representing different religious groups and confessions (beginning with the 17th century up to the 1980s they were mostly Christians or originated from so-called Christian countries). The CGM was born in the very depths of American individualism and was immediately accepted by much of the middle class. As a result, the emphasis was put on individual decisions. Each person for him/her decides on the religious beliefs and the denomination or the church that could satisfy his/her spiritual hunger. Quite differently, the Orthodox Church, which has been for centuries shaping the world outlook of the majority of Eastern European inhabitants, places emphasis on community.

The CGM especially emphasizes the salvation of the human soul, and for this reason, all good works of charity, and projects that are even more social, are related to an individual decision. A person may carry out charity work or not, but this does not define the degree of his spirituality or maturity. Money is required not for charity in the first place but for the achievement of evangelistic projects, short and long-term missionary trips and planting of new churches. The Orthodox Church cannot accept such an approach, since there is salvation not only of the human soul, but of the human being as a whole, of mankind, of all creation. The charity works are an indication of spiritual maturity and even faith.

The purpose of the CGM mission is the enrolment of followers ready to plant new churches which will become independent and self-governed. In contrast to the Orthodox Church, the unity issue is discussed only at the level of individual congregations. In all other aspects each individual community has every right to self-determination and to choose its own path of development. Most churches and denominations that follow this missionary paradigm are not part of the ecumenical movement, do not consider it necessary to participate in joint projects, and regard cautiously (and sometimes aggressively) people of other faiths.

The indicator of a mission's effectiveness is the number of new communities and followers. The Orthodox Church does not count the people coming to worship, and the ultimate goal of its mission is the *theosis*, deification of human beings, when people can become as God. Such a mission starts during the life of a single person as well as of a people in general, and continues after people's death through the prayers of the people remaining on earth.

The starting point of the missionary activity of the church from the point of view of the CGM is the spiritual gifts and the apostolic example of St. Paul, while the Orthodox Church has been viewing for many centuries God the Father as leading Sender, and the Son and the Spirit as envoys. Based on the foregoing, it may give the impression that they do not have any common ground. In fact, a few common things can be identified in both positions.

The first, as well as the second concept accentuate the central role of Jesus Christ in the Church's activity, the salvation of human beings and mission. Additionally, in both cases the role of the local community should be noted. People are invited to attend the church and from there they are sent into the world to serve. Serving refers to different concepts, as already mentioned, but the role of community involvement is extremely high in the formation of a Christian.

Orthodox Missiology Vis-a-vis the Lausanne Movement

The so-called post-imperial paradigm took shape at the time when many former colonies had obtained their independence (the 1960s and 1970s). Accordingly, this had a big impact not only on the political world, but also on the religious world. The voice of the Third World countries (as they used to be called) began to be heard. It was speaking about the poverty and injustice prevailing there, the oppression and famine, war and disease. It was saying that the Church should not engage in evangelism while nearby thousands of children were dying and their deaths could be prevented. Nevertheless, one of the Lausanne movement goals was the evangelization of the whole world (Chapter 4, point 2). Unlike the CGM, the social responsibility not only of individual Christians, but also of the local communities, denominations and interdenominational organizations began to play an important role in the mission of the church. "Evangelical theology of mission today encompasses more than just evangelistic proclamation, but includes also much of what traditionally would have been called 'good works' or the 'social gospel'. This touches on what is perhaps the most difficult topic to work through, the relationship between mission and evangelism."[5]

Lausanne was not talking about the salvation of the whole creation; the dualistic worldview was receding into the past. People were spoken of as holistic personalities without functionally separating body, mind and soul. Despite the use of similar terminology, Orthodoxy means something different when speaking about the integrity of salvation. Integrity for Orthodoxy means continuity of people concerning their culture, land and ancestral heritage. A person is seen as an indivisible part of an indivisible whole. On the other hand, the Lausanne movement, speaking of integrity, called the church to pay attention not only to the spiritual, but also to the physical

---

[5] Tim Grass (ed). 2001. *Evangelicalism and the Orthodox Church. A Report by the Evangelical Alliance (UK), Commission on the Unity and Truth among Evangelicals.* (ACUTE) Carlisle: Paternoster, p.136.

needs of people, increasingly giving preference to the spiritual needs, namely the need of hearing the Good News.

There is a certain similarity between the Lausanne movement and the Orthodox Church. Almost from the very beginning, missiologists and theologians participating in the Lausanne dialogue were developing a Trinitarian theology as the foundation for the Church's mission. Although the Orthodox understanding of *perichoresis* uses a completely different methodology to explain the relationship within the Trinity, the similarity lies in the fact that the doctrine of the Trinity is not valuable just from the apologetic point of view, but serves as a real basis for the life and the ministry of the Church.

Another distinctive feature is the ability to communicate with the representatives of other denominations and churches. The Lausanne Movement itself is a movement, where participants represent many Evangelical traditions. As stated in the Manila Manifesto in 1989:

> Our reference to "the whole church" is not a presumptuous claim. The universal church and the evangelical community are synonymous. For we recognize, that there are many churches which are not part of the evangelical movement. Evangelical attitude to the Roman Catholic and Orthodox Churches differs widely. Some evangelicals are praying, talking, studying Scripture and working with these churches. Others are strongly opposed to any form of dialogue or cooperation with them. All are aware that serious theological differences between us remain. Where appropriate, and so long as biblical truth is not compromised, cooperation may be possible in such areas as Bible translation, the study of contemporary theological and ethics issues, social work and political action; we wish to make it clear, however, that common evangelism demands a common commitment to the biblical gospel.[6]

> Evangelicals value unity and fellowship among Christians for more effective witness of the gospel and to foster interpersonal relationships of common faith, trust, and prayer, rather than relying on organizational or hierarchical structures.[7]

At the same time, open theological discussions are held with Orthodox theologians in order to carry out joint evangelistic work. Some churches supporting the Lausanne movement are at the same time part of the World Council of Churches and other ecumenical organisations.

Although it looks like there are more differences than similarities, this does not mean that further dialogue is impossible. Conversation should go forward, but taking in consideration that the Lausanne movement was not well known in Moldova, it might be that Moldavian Evangelicals can find another platform for fruitful discussion with Orthodoxy.

---

[6] Francis A. Oborji. 2006. *Concepts of Mission: the Evolution of the Contemporary Missiology* (Maryknoll, NY: Orbis Books), 170.

[7] Ibid, 168.

Orthodox Missiology Vis-a-vis the Anabaptist Movement

In comparison with the previous two approaches, as strange as it may seem, the approach of the Anabaptists is seen favourably in the eyes of the Orthodoxy. Modern Anabaptism, as well as Orthodoxy, does not use the term 'evangelism', or the meaning behind it. Both prefer to use the word 'witness', referring to the spread of the Good News to the world. Both of them pay special attention to witness by their way of life, as opposed to active evangelism which follows the two previous approaches. Also, it is interesting to mention that Anabaptists do not try to determine the degree of their effectiveness by quantitative growth. In this regard they are also similar to the Orthodox. Furthermore, both view efficiency as being determined by the degree of people's obedience to God.

Mission is based on Trinitarian theology and the vision is theocentric. However, not all contemporary theologians put the same meaning into this concept. Anabaptist theologians do not aim to describe the ontological relationship between the three persons of the Trinity, as did the Fathers of the Church and the Orthodox theologians of the 19th and 20th centuries. Anabaptists, as mentioned above, stepped into the existing dialogue on this subject enriching it with good deeds and charity. Most Anabaptists believe in the significant role of good works in the rescue process. This is their particular resemblance to Orthodoxy, which has a similar concept about synergetic work with God. Despite the fact that repentance has a beginning, it does not end in this life on earth. The whole of human life is a process of rethinking the relationship with God and with people. This does not diminish or depreciate the role of Jesus Christ and that of His sacrifice on Calvary. Both Anabaptists and Orthodox argue that salvation is possible through faith only, and faith is the starting point of the Christian life. But the future life consolidates and confirms the chosen path.

It is also necessary to note the role of the community and the church. For Anabaptists ethics (spirituality – in Orthodox language) are not the personal choice of every individual, but the responsibility of the entire community.

Anabaptist communities pay special attention to the role of the community in the education of each believer. It may seem that in Eastern Europe this is the consequence of the Soviet era when people were also educated collectively. But the Mennonites in Germany, the USA and Canada still use the same methods. "The aim of the meeting of the church members, for instance, is to find together the mind of Christ who is present in the midst of His church, and to use the scriptures to help us in this search for His purpose in our world today."[8] People in the community have a relatively close relationship, and collectively help each other in following Christ and in compliance with the rules of conduct and the standards of the church.

> From their earliest days, Baptists did not insist on the 'independence' of the local church, but rather the direct dependence of the local church on the authority of Christ … But on the other hand, because the aim of the local church members was to discover Christ's purpose for them, they gladly affirmed that they needed

---

[8] Ibid., 16.

the counsel and insight of other Christian congregations who made up the one Body of Christ, and with whom they lived in covenant relationship.[9]

Though the majority of Orthodox parishes in Eastern Europe rarely practice the same forms of education and discipline as Anabaptists, group thinking clearly dominates individual choice. Anabaptists have their own vision of the concept of *Missio Dei*. W. Shenk supposes that Jesus' self-understanding issued directly from the *Missio Dei*.[10]

When thinking about the differences, one of the most difficult issues is to understand the unity of the Church. Anabaptists, as well as representatives of the Church Growth Movement stress the unity of Christians of one and the same community and faith although they are making their first steps in theological debates, initiating dialogues with the ecumenical community, the Lausanne movement, and the Orthodox Church. The issue of the unity of the Church is not the key in the mission of these groups as it is for the Orthodox Church. Nevertheless, in recent times, believers deny 'aggressive evangelism' and proselytism. "If Baptist evangelists try to proselytise among active members of other Christian churches for the purpose of increasing the numbers of the Baptist denomination, they fail to fulfil their calling."[11]

---

[9]   Ibid., 17.

[10] Wilbert A. Shenk. 2007. 'Crossing Frontiers', in Shenk, Wilbert R. and Penner, Peter F. (eds.), *Anabaptism and Mission* (Neufeld Verlag), 26.

[11] E. Geldbach. 1999. 'Religious Liberty, Proselytism, Evangelism. Some Baptists Considerations', in Cupit, T. *Baptist Faith & Witness. Book Two. The papers of the Study and Research Division of the Baptist World Alliance 1995-2000* (Baptist World Alliance), 28.

Comparative Analysis of All Paradigms

Having studied these missiological paradigms and comparing them to the paradigm of the Orthodox mission, we are going to present the results schematically to make them easier to understand.

	Church Growth Movement	Lausanne Movement	Anabaptist Movement	Orthodox Church
World View	Individualistic	Individualistic	Corporate	Corporate
Foundation for mission	Theology of St. Paul	Trinitarian	Trinitarian	Trinitarian
Goal of mission	New disciples and churches	Evangelization of the whole world	Preaching the Gospel	*Theosis*
Mission's approach	Evangelism	Holistic	Witness	Holistic, witness
Unity	In particular congregation	Among all Evangelicals. Dialogue with the others	Congregation, denomination	Among all Christians in Orthodox Church
Participation in social ministry	No	Yes, partly	Yes	Yes
View on Proselytism	Not important	Sensitive	Sensitive	Painful
View on Canonical territory	Absence of this concept	Absence of this concept	Absence of this concept	Strict
Presence of Missio Dei concept	No	Yes	Yes	Yes, implicitly

Thus, it is obvious that the CGM approach is the most inadequate in the Orthodox context. It causes the greatest number of controversial issues, conflicts with the Orthodox Church and creates contentious comments. It has nothing in common with Orthodoxy and on many issues is opposed to the representatives of other Evangelical paradigms. The only issue on which the CGM, Lausanne and Anabaptists agree is the issue of canonical territory. All of them reject this idea, and most of the ecumenical missiologists think that this teaching is not relevant in a contemporary, globalized post-modern world.

Concerning the rest of the approaches, three paradigms have three points out of ten in common with the Orthodox Church: the presence of the *Missio Dei* concept, participation in social ministry and foundation for mission. They also refer with consideration to the pain the Orthodox Church feels in regard to proselytism. Speaking about vision of the world, Anabaptists are closer to the Orthodox than anyone else. As for the goal of mission and the issue of unity, the ecumenical paradigm has more in common with the Orthodox Church than all the rest.

Misunderstanding of God's Mission Causes Struggles in Adopting New Mission Concepts

The main question in this area deals with how to determine what the Father is doing. History has proven that quite often churches have had a wrong understanding of the mission of God, His purposes, methods and tasks set before the church. S.K. George considers that all that the church calls 'mission' may not be God's work. It is easy to have mixed motivations and to present one's own personal and cultural projects and advancement as though they were God's.[12]

It seems to us that the most correct understanding of what God wants from the church can be inferred from what God values. The values marked by the Triune God must serve as our guiding lines in defining the mission of the church.

"If the world is so much the arena of God's activity, then Christians must think of the world as a key arena of their service. Trinitarian mission would include involvement in the world, whereby Christians seek to uphold God's values (some would say 'kingdom values')."[13] The following continues the thought: "in a world where so many people are 'blind' to the values of God's reign of peace and justice, where the forces of death and violence seem to prevail over life, we must seek, recognize, and join 'God's works'."[14] "Wherever injustice is opposed, racism is rebuked, ignorance is dispelled, healing is experienced, and reconciliation takes place, there the frontiers of evil are driven back, the kingdom comes and the transforming mission of God proceeds on its way."[15]

By discussing the subject of God's values, the kingdom and the church, it is impossible not to pay attention to the contribution that the representatives of liberation theology have made to modern theology. As Gustavo Gutiérrez said: "It is the task of the church to bear witness to this dwelling and this new world (Rev 21:1-4); in this way it proclaims the kingdom in which the Lord makes himself present in human history."[16]

Throughout many years similar discussions have been going on; and we cannot say they have ceased nowadays. It is encouraging that within the last twenty years theologians and missiologists have begun to listen to each other more than in the 1960s.

---

[12] Sherron K. George. 2004. *Called as Partners in Christ's Service.* (Westminster: John Knox Press), 7.

[13] Ajith Fernando. 2000. 'God: the Source, the Originator, and the End of Mission', in Taylor, W.D. (ed.), *Global Missiology for the 21ˢᵗ Century: the Iguassu Dialogue* (Grand Rapids, MI: Baker Academic), 198.

[14] George, *Called as Partners in Christ's Service*, 10.

[15] Roy Williamson. 1996. *For Such a Time as This: Sharing in the Mission of God Today.* (Darton: Longman & Todd), 62.

[16] Gustavo Gutiérrez. 1991. *The God of Life* (E.T. by M.J. O'Connell; Maryknoll, NY: Orbis Books), 106.

There are clear signs of dialogue. However, we have to note here that today's trends among Evangelicals are drastically different from those of the previous generation. The works written by evangelical missiologists during the last decade have been putting more and more emphasis on the social ministry of the church, on getting involved with the needs of the community.

Misunderstanding of 'The World' Causes Struggles in Adopting New Mission Concepts

We can find in the Bible words that the church should be separated from the world, but the problem is that we mix such concepts as 'world/sin' and 'world/community/society'. The Christian majority still criticizes the WCC statement that "the World dictates the agenda for the Church", and, in their criticism, they say that the Church has to react to the needs of the society. In my understanding, reaction to needs is quite similar to the adoption of a plan. If the needs of the world determine the areas of church ministry, then consequently, the world determines these areas, at least those that have to do with the social ministry of the church. We cannot state that there are certain 'worldly' structures that are working to make a 'plan' for the church; rather, this is the answer to certain historical processes. Discussing these issues, we recognize that behind the history of the world there is God – the Lord of the entire universe. From this, it follows that God himself initiates at least part of these processes, and consequently, He – God – dictates the 'agenda for the World'. God draws the attention of the church to the world through His plan.

Thus, by reacting to the historical situation, to the needs of the society in which the church is located, the church follows God's plan, if, of course, it uses God's methods in doing this.

Misunderstanding of the mission's centre causes struggles in adopting new mission concepts

Besides the debate regarding the 'plan' there are talks about the 'centre of the mission'. Various models are offered here – Christ-centred, Theo-centred, Church-centred, etc. A. Kirk observes:

> During the last half century, a vigorous debate has been joined within the Church on the relationship between the *Missio Dei*, the Church and the world. There have been times in the past when Christians assumed that all God's purposes would be fulfilled exclusively through the Church. There have been theologies which have either identified the kingdom completely with the Church or which have regarded the kingdom as a purely future event. A Church-centred missiology undergirded the extraordinary missionary thrust of the last two centuries, with its emphasis on the planting of self-supporting, self-governing and self-propagating churches, although perhaps the 'civilizing' aspect of the mission reflected some kind of (distorted) reference to the kingdom.[17]

---

[17] J. Andrew Kirk. 2000. *What is Mission?* (Augsburg Fortress Publ.), 33.

Many people today are talking about the need for radical changes in the church, about a 'radical mission'. "Being a prophetic presence through a radical biblical community life may be one of the biggest challenges facing the church in the 21st century."[18] "On the practical level this means that the Church is to be a radical presence in society. It is always putting itself in true repentance wholly into God's hands, submitting to God's revealed will in Scripture and trusting in His mercy."[19] "If the Church is to pursue and maintain an effective and radical mission towards the nation, seeking the nation's true health and wholeness through a prophetic ministry of the Word of God, it must also open itself to the necessity for radical repentance, reform and renewal."[20] "A Church under the cross should be the exact opposite of an introverted and contemplative company. It should be a Church *for* the world."[21] "The essential Church is never the same during any two days, because it is constantly becoming, developing, and 'emerging'. Yet in another sense the Church is already by nature what it is becoming and simply must continually change, improve, reform and emerge."[22]

Then "mission calls us to a radical re-examination. If mission is a part of the essence of the Church's nature as the body of Christ and the people of God, then it ought to be at the top of the list."[23] As Yoder mentioned:

> Our fundamental observation was that through most of the history of the Christian church, the geographical and numeral expansion of Christianity was the result not of separately organized, centrally administrated, and externally financed missionary specialists. It came through normal, often unplanned, usually self-supporting movements of Christians who took their living faith with them as they moved with their sources of livelihood.[24]

Talking about the purpose of the church, Kirk explained it well using the following words: "To clarify the nature of mission is to answer the question, what is the Church for? It is entirely for the purposes for which God called it into being. It was a community in response to the *Missio Dei*, bearing witness to God's activity in the world by its communication of the good news of Jesus Christ in word and deed."[25]

---

[18] Ajith Fernando. 'The Church: the mirror of the Trinity' in Taylor, W.D. (ed.), *Global Missiology for the 21st Century: the Iguassu Dialogue*. (Grand Rapids, MI: Baker Academic), 255.

[19] Arthur Glasser, Charles Van Engen, Gilliland and Redford. 2003. *Announcing the Kingdom: the Story of God's mission in the Bible*. (Mi: Baker Academic), 340.

[20] Roy Williamson, *For Such as Time as This*, 66.

[21] R. Thadden. 1953. 'The Church Under the Cross', in Goodall, N. (ed.), *Missions Under the Cross*: addresses delivered at the Enlarged Meeting of the Committee of the International Missionary Council at Willingen, in Germany, 1952 (International Missionary Council, Edinburgh House Press), 62.

[22] Charles e. van Engen. 1991. *God's Missionary People: Rethinking the Purpose of the Local Church*. (Grand Rapids, MI: Baker Book House), 41.

[23] Ibid., 80.

[24] John Howard Yoder. 1961. *As You Go: the Old Mission in a New Day*. (Scottdale, PA: Herald Press), 17.

[25] Kirk. *What is Mission?*, 31.

"One may say that we are in danger of perpetuating 'come-structures' instead of re-placing them by 'go-structures'."[26] The replacement of structures throughout history has been accompanied by pain and often big loss. But today, the church has practi-cally no choice. Faced by the many challenges in the world today, the church has indeed to reconsider its tasks and structures.

Misunderstanding of Kenotic Way Causes Struggles in Adopting New Mission Concepts

It is impossible to reconsider the structures without a deep re-thinking of its mission, its role in the divine plan and its purpose. Jesus Christ said: "as the Father has sent me, I am sending you." (Jn 20:21). The Church has been sent in the same way as the Son was sent. The sending model of the Son was discussed above. First, the Son was sent into the world; second, the Son was sent to preach the approaching of the king-dom; third, the Son was sent to be the approaching kingdom. Thus, the church is sent into the world, the church is sent to preach the values of the Kingdom, the church is sent to be the sign of the Kingdom. "God so loved the world that he gave his one and only Son, that whoever believes in him shall not perish but have eternal life" (Jn 3:16). The Father gave away His dearest. The Son, in His turn, loved this world so much, that He gave away the dearest thing He had – His 'Body' (His Church) to testify about Him. God the Father gives away His possession for the sake of the world; God the Son gives away what He has. The church is given to the world for the sake of the world's salvation. "The church, in the power of the Spirit, is also God's gift to the world because the church is the body of Christ, of whom Christ himself is head. The church embraces its identity and pursues the *Missio Dei* in as much as and precisely to the extent that the church bears witness in its life to the grace of God in Christ and lives."[27]

"*Missio Dei* pushes us beyond ourselves and our familiar routines. The church exists toward and for the world."[28] As L. Newbigin has said: "… mission changes not only the world but also the church."[29] "The *Missio Dei* is *missio ecclesiae*… the *missio ecclesiae* is not the *Missio Dei*. Mission cannot be something the community pos-sesses, for it is not the community in isolation. It is this living fellowship in which the divine retains the initiative and the community lives in response. This ordered identity means that the community must be active by the Spirit in following her Lord into the world."[30]

---

[26] Final Report of the Western European Working Group and North American Working Group of the Department on Studies in Evangelism, 19.

[27] Michael Jinkins. "The Gift of the Church: Ecclesia Crucis, Peccatrix Maxima, and the Missio Dei," in *Evangelical Ecclesiology: Reality or Illusion?* ed. John G. Stackhouse, Jr. (Grand Rapids: Baker Academics, 2003), 206.

[28] George. *Called as Partners in Christ's Service*, 92.

[29] Lesslie Newbigin. 1995. *The Open Secret: An Introduction to the Theology of Mission.* (Grand Rap-ids: William B. Eerdmans), 59.

[30] John G. Flett. 2010. *The Witness of God: The Trinity, Missio Dei, Karl Barth, and the Nature of Christian Community.* (Grand Rapids: William B. Eerdmans), 291.

Misunderstanding of Christian Unity Causes Struggles in Adopting New Mission Concepts

Church unity is also part of the mission of God. In other words, the mission of God can be carried out only when there is unity. "The concept of *Missio Dei* might in future become a point of convergence, after having contributed to past divisions."[31] Further: "We should develop the *Missio Dei* concept, even if we use it only as a metaphor for God's love and presence, unconditional availability, as well as God's unknown aspects … It makes sense to begin any reflection on the matter with those aspects of God's mission which we do know, i.e. with *Missio Christi*, mission in Christ's way."[32]

We should try to find common points in God's mission, even if we experienced failures in the past. The comparison between business and mission, which was made by Theo Sundermeier, appears to be very interesting for us: "Cultural, economic and social differences are rarely enough taken seriously in business life. Because they are played down or ignored, 70% of joint ventures fail. Ecumenical relations also often fail because cultural, social and spiritual differences are underestimated. That is why the idea of partnership has to be enriched by that of friendship. Partners must become friends. Only where true friendships arise through and from congregational partnership, be they between single persons, a few families or special church groups, will such partnerships succeed and survive through the years even in spite of difficulties and tensions. Partners seek equality, and depend on the same interests and tasks, but friends enjoy differences and preserve the distance that is the space of freedom."[33]

Further: "anyone who does not change is dominant and only tries to change the others they meet, and that has nothing to do with mission."[34]

Holistic and dynamic approaches in mission mean openness of the churches to listen to each other, and altogether listening to the world. If we defined that God speaks to the world not only through the Church, it means that it is possible to hear His voice through the world. From my understanding, this is the only way today to be heard by the world, because by listening to the world the Church will be allowed to speak to the world.

Conclusion

The responsibility of any local church is to try to find its part in the Universal Church, in her mission, in *Missio Dei*, to spread the Gospel of the Lord Jesus Christ in the power of the Holy Spirit with the goal that all people will subordinate themselves to the will of God in His kingdom, which is among them, with shalom in their hearts. Every local church is responsible for finding her mission in unity with the other Christian traditions and local churches with the hope that one day all Christians from the all nations and generations will praise the Triune God in the eternal kingdom of God.

---

[31] Jacques Matthey. 2003. 'God's Mission Today: Summary and Conclusions.' in *IRM*, Vol. 92, No. 367, 581.

[32] Ibid.

[33] Theo Sundermeier. 2003. 'Missio Dei Today', in *IRM*, Vol. 92, No. 367, 564.

[34] Ibid., 566.

Martin Robinson, Gabriel Stängle[1]

Missional –
The New Paradigm in Our Heterogeneous Contexts

When one uses the word *missional*, sometimes, instead of providing clarifications and answers, the very word seems to raise numerous questions. *Missional* – is it more than a new buzzword, or a "code word for a claim to the moral high ground" in missiological debates (Richardson 2013:131)? What is the difference between *missionary* and *missional*? Does adding an *al* to the end of mission create a new meaning? "Yes", argue Alan Roxburgh and Scott Boren: "The word invites us to stop, check our assumptions, and ask if there might be a different way of being the church" (Roxburgh/Boren 2009:30). If missional is not about doing but more about being, what does it mean to have the *Missio Dei* at the core of the church's identity? We are told that the missional church is opposing everything that has to do with the "attractional model" of church planting. But it is easier to define what is *not* meant by missional than to say what the word means: at least ... no models, no definitions, no programmes, no denomination (Roxburgh/Boren 2009:27-39).

Others argue that "in many cases, the phrase *missional church* simply puts new clothes on old trends, such as the seeker-sensitive church movement, the church-growth movement, and so on" (Billings 2008:56). Quite a number of people are sceptical about whether the word has a different meaning at all. That is maybe one reason the German translators of Michael Frost's and Alan Hirsch's *The shaping of the things to come* refused to use the term *missional* arguing that it would sound "awkward" (Frost/Hirsch 2008:357). Others fear that missionary zeal and activity might be lost. The German evangelist Ulrich Parzany, being suspicious of missional language, asks "We are becoming missional – and the evangelistic ministries are crossed off the list!?" (Parzany 2013). In many cases missional is becoming a pure container-term meaning everything and nothing at the same time. This is especially true where it just replaces the term *missionary* because this is seen old and odd in contrast to the in-term missional. Rick Richardson on the other hand insists that "Missional churches move toward challenging the secular, individualistic, consumer-oriented, therapeutic-style, business-imitating, market-driven, building-dominated church of the West. They seek to model an alternative kingdom community oriented toward service and mission and to be the incarnation-like extension of Jesus' ministry, values, and presence into the world" (Richardson 2013:131). Missional is often used by missiologists and theologians when they speak about times of massive tran-

---

[1] Martin Robinson, PhD in Mission, Revd. Principal of Springdale College and Chief Executive Officer of Together in Mission. Springdale College is the institution where he teaches and Springdale offers degrees validated by the University of York St John. Gabriel Stängle, M.Th. (UNISA), teaches English, History, Religious Education, Geography and Social Sciences at the Christiane-Herzog-Realschule, Nagold (Germany). Member of the Advisory Board of Operation Mobilisation (OM), Germany.

sition.[2] We are in a post-era where we realise that the things that are regarded as a matter of course are gone and that there are many more questions than answers. This goes together with massive shifts in Western culture. But what is even more challenging is the diversification of our lifeworld and the question of how to respond to that as a church and as an individual.

Let us have a look at the contemporary tale of Hans and Peter. Take Hans first. He represents a citizen of the world many of us grew up with, or at least are familiar with. Hans lives in the medium-sized town of Bensheim in Hesse, where he was born. He has a nine-to-five-job as a clerk in a local sales company. His parish church is two blocks away. His girlfriend and most of his friends are part of a dynamic youth group. Hans is regularly involved in missionary outreach to the homeless and neglected people of his town. Being missional? No problem most people would argue. He is on a missional path.

But how should one be missional when neighbourhood, leisure time, workplace, marriage & family and the community don't meet anymore? At the annual meeting of the German Association of Evangelical Missiology (AfeM) Gabriel argued three years ago that we have to find answers to the challenge of the plurality of lifeworld (Stängle 2011:113-114).

Take Peter, who lives in Berlin. He works in an international IT-company. He connects online with his project partners who are situated in Birmingham, Göteborg and Barcelona. His fiancée is studying in Hamburg. Two friends of his former Bible study group study in Canada or work in Singapore. Most of his spiritual dialogues are on the web where he also receives a lot of inspiration. He is part of a group who takes care of asylum seekers in a local church nearby. What about normal church life? That question produces a negative report. On the weekend, he is in Hamburg. How can one be missional in these social-cultural space(s) which lack any significant physical connection?

As the above discussion reveals, the word missional and the debate that surrounds it produces many further questions and dilemmas. In order to understand why this might be the case, it is helpful to return to the origins of the terms missional. In fact this word is properly located in a broader discussion about mission and its meaning. That discussion was given a particular direction and energy.

A Short Sketch about the History of "Missional"

The Starting Point of the *Missio Dei*

Karl Barth was the first theologian of the 20th century who said the concept of *missio* in the early church is to be found in the Trinity. It is an activity of the "divine self-mission, the mission of the Son and of the Holy Spirit into the world" (Barth 1957:115 Gabriel's translation). The term *Missio Dei* was coined by Karl Harten-

---

[2] If we believe the latest statistics, we will witness the end of the established churches in Germany's strongest evangelical and catholic region, Baden-Württemberg, in the year 2040, in: Stuttgarter Nachrichten 15.10.2010, in: http://www.stuttgarter-nachrichten.de/inhalt.der-traditionelle-glaube-liegt-im-sterben.ee78410e-5312-4e19-a506-9c4fe4f7bfc7.html (27.12.2011).

stein, a prelate in the Evangelical Lutheran Church of Württemberg, in a reflection on the IMC-conference at Willingen in 1952. He wrote: "Mission is not a matter of human activity or organization, 'its source is the triune God himself'. The mission of the Son for the reconciliation of all things through the power of the Spirit is the foundation and goal of the mission. Only from the *Missio Dei* can the *Missio Ecclesia* emerge. Mission has been placed in the broadest possible context of salvation history and God's plan of salvation." (Hartenstein 1952:62 – Gabriel's translation). *Missio Dei* locates the source of mission in the triune God, not in ecclesiology or soteriology. The starting point of mission is not a human endeavour but an attribute of the Trinity. Hartenstein broadened the *Missio Dei* concept to include the church in God's mission. Hartenstein goes on: "There is no participation in Christ without participation in his mission to the world. (...) Mission reveals the deepest purpose of the church as God's mission to/of all humanity, the first fruit of salvation. Talking rightly about the church means to talk about its mission to the world. The church exists in its mission." (Hartenstein 1952:63 – Gabriel's translation). Central to all missional thinking and the missional church is the participation of God's people in the *Missio Dei,* and the idea that God's mission permeates all actions of church life. Lesslie Newbigin was a key person involved in the Willingen conference and he developed these themes further when he came back to his home in England following retirement as a missionary from India.

Lesslie Newbigin and the Gospel and Our Culture Network

The story of Lesslie Newbigin's return from his work as a missionary in India to his home in England and then his subsequent missionary encounter with Western culture is well told in a number of publications, not least by Newbigin himself in his small volume, *The Other Side of 1984* (Newbigin 1983). The important element in his return from a lifetime of missionary service was the very painful realisation that the culture he knew prior to his departure to India – a broadly Christian culture – had largely disappeared by the time of his return. The transformation of Western culture in that relatively short period of time was dramatic and far-reaching, so much so that it required an explanation. He wanted to know what had taken place to cause the founding story of the West to lose its influence, to become profoundly marginalised in such a relatively short time.[3]

---

[3] What is less known is Newbigin's involvement in the Oxford *Faith and Order Conference* of 1937. As a young Theology student of some promise, Newbigin had been recruited by one of the pioneers of the *Edinburgh Missionary* Conference of 1910, John Mott, to help him organize one of the most important British conferences of the first half of the 20th century. Mott was also one of the leading lights in the ecumenical movement and acted as an important mentor to the young Newbigin. The background was the perceived fracturing of Christendom following the tragedy of the First World War, and the profound challenge that had arisen, particularly for the churches of Europe, from the twin political movements of Communism and Fascism. Mott was trying to see how the churches might overcome their loss of influence in an emerging new period of industrialisation and mass social movements that had lost their earlier connections with Christianity. That earlier background helped to shape Newbigin's thinking in relation to his own reflections on the relationship between Christianity and Western culture in the second half of the 20th century. The connecting factor had been his personal involvement in missions and the ecumenical movement. One of the fruits of that journey had been the uniting of the *International Missionary Council* with the *World Council of Churches*. As a partial consequence of the marriage of these two institutions, Newbigin was exposed

Newbigin's analysis of the situation started in earnest after he took up a post in retirement, teaching at the Selly Oak Colleges – a federation of missionary colleges, located in south Birmingham. According to his own account, he was struck by a question from a leading Indonesian layperson, "Can the West be converted?" That was a deeply provocative question to ask of a former missionary from the West. The issue was no longer, how one might increase the influence of the church, or how the church might be more effective in converting westerners but rather, is it even possible for the West to be converted. The point being that this was possibly the first time in human history that a whole culture had voluntarily abandoned its own founding narrative. From the perspective of that Indonesian layperson, it was much more difficult to convert those who had already rejected a narrative compared with taking the story to those who were hearing it for the first time.

Newbigin's important contribution to this debate was based on his analysis that Christianity was not facing the absence of faith so much as the assault of another faith. That faith was not Islam, Hinduism, or one of the other great world faiths as much as a new faith, one that had partly been birthed by Christianity, namely Western secular thought. To name the child of the Enlightenment a faith with its own internal belief system was incisive as a piece of analysis but also helpful in beginning to create an apologetic approach that Christians might begin to develop. In many ways, to name secular thought a faith and not the sole arbiter of what constituted faith, pretending to be somehow above faith, created something of a level playing field. Newbigin pointed out that there is no neutral space. All is contested space. No longer could secular thought claim to be the owner of public space with Christianity relegated to the world of private belief or opinion. All could claim to contribute to the public square. What remained was for Christianity to consider how to speak into the public space because the old ways of doing that which had belonged to Christendom, no longer worked.

The Gospel and *Our Culture* Programme

The response to *The Other Side of 1984* and its subsequent volume, *Foolishness to the Greeks* (1986), encouraged Newbigin, in close collaboration with his fellow retired missionary and lecturer at Selly Oak, Dan Beeby, to establish the Gospel and *Our Culture* programme. The focus for this programme was a series of "pods" consisting of leading Christian thinkers in key areas of culture, who would offer a Christian critique of these subject areas. These findings would be brought to a large national conference to be held at Swanwick, England, in 1992.[4] The immediate impact

---

very directly to the way in which secular thought had impacted theology in general and the ecumenical movement in particular. It was a painful experience for Newbigin and helped him to ask some very penetrating questions about what was taking place both in the church and in Western culture and more directly in the interplay between these two realities.

[4] The model for this process and for the conference itself was the *Oxford Faith and Order Conference* of 1937. The British and Foreign Bible Society was a key partner in the Swanwick event. They helped to pay for the event and provided an administrative team to ensure it took place. It was not necessarily clear to the participants at the Swanwick event where the model had been drawn from. Had it been made more explicit there might have been more questions about the model. However, it is by no means clear what other models might have been used at that time because thinking about how the churches might relate to Western culture in a post Christendom situation had not really taken place in earnest prior to the Swanwick conference. In some ways Swanwick 1992 did not achieve

was to establish an ongoing *Gospel and Our Culture network* in the UK and a few other nations in Europe together with places such as New Zealand. A more significant group with the title *Gospel and Culture* (the 'Our' element was dropped), was established in North America and for a time was considerably more active than groups in any other area or nation. There was no attempt to connect the various regional or national networks and so the sense of a broader movement was probably lost in the post-Swanwick era. The death of Newbigin in 1998 and the illness of his co-worker Dan Beeby at the same time caused the earlier momentum to be lost, particularly in the United Kingdom but also more widely.

In North America, apart from a number of annual conferences, the most visible outcome was the publication of a book edited by Darrell Guder, *The Missional Church: A Vision for the Sending of the Church in North America* (1998). This volume was significant in two respects apart from the immediate content of its pages. First, it adopted the word "missional", which was largely a new construct, in order to overcome the perceived difficulty that for churches in the West, the word "mission" always meant overseas mission. The word "missional" was coined to help the churches of the West to take their immediate context more seriously. Second, the book inadvertently turned the missional debate into a discussion on ecclesiology. In other words, the debate with culture was to a large extent lost. To a certain extent, participants in the missional discussion began to focus on a discussion about models of church. They were addressing the question as to what kind of church would be required for mission in the West to be effective. That was not a helpful turn.

Missional Streams – The Current Situation

From the writings of Lesslie Newbigin and the *Gospel and our Culture Network* grew what we call the *missional conversation* or different missional streams. Leaders and theologians such as Darrell Guder, George Hunsberger, Lois Barrett, Craig Van Gelder and Alan Roxburgh began calling for a missional and prophetic engagement with Western culture. They have had a huge influence on the other missional streams as well as on the whole missiological debate. Out of that a number of different streams developed (Richardson 2013.131-133):

The first one is *the emerging stream*. It is also sometimes referred to as the *emerging missional church*. These are young leaders from the UK, the US and Australia who have engaged in postmodern culture since the 1990s. Important figures in that movement are Brian McLaren, Tony Jones, Dan Kimball, Nadia Bolz-Weber, Mark Driscoll and others. The emerging church movement has fragmented into different directions:

---

a great deal. There was a good quality of debate but little clarity about how that debate might be carried forward. Arguably, there was a diffuse effect in that significant numbers of thinkers did begin to consider some of the larger questions that Newbigin had raised through the Swanwick / *Gospel and Our Culture* process. Many writers acknowledge their debt to Newbigin and although that debt might have been accumulated through reading his books, the *Gospel and Our Culture* process, centring as it did on Swanwick, gave a sense that this was a broader movement and not just a series of books.

❑ Dan Kimball and Marc Driscoll are representatives of the *relevants,* a stream of the emergent church which can be described as theologically conservative but culturally innovative and liberal.

❑ *Reconstructionists* such as Darrell Guder and George Hunsberger are not just redefining strategies but they also try to redefine ecclesiology with a strong Anabaptist flavour. Here the church is seen as an alternative community. The Australians Michael Frost and Alan Hirsch (Frost/Hirsch 2003) place a strong focus on an incarnational theology and agenda.

❑ "*Revisionists* are rethinking the basic theology and ethics of the church, using more postmodern, socially constructionist epistemologies and operate with greater awareness of social location and social power" (Richardson 2013:132). Brian McLaren is the most popular among the emergent revisionists. He and many others have caused a great debate among Evangelicals because they questioned some key Protestant understandings such as the atonement, the role of the cross or the authority of scripture.

The streams of the emerging church and the missional church movement are sometimes freely mixed together. Both have similar shared interests in that they form a milieu of how questions are raised and discussed. One of the major differences is of biographical nature. Many of the leading missional thinkers are academics, belonging to mainline denominations. Many of the contributors in the emerging stream are Low Church Protestants (Doornenbaal 2012:2-7).

The *multi-ethnic stream* comprises many urban, multi-ethnic oriented churches which "are embracing a Gospel based on the theology of the kingdom that sees evangelism, justice and reconciliation as the core of the Gospel" (Richardson 2013:132).

The *neo-monastic stream* has a strong interest in global justice issues. Often they form new communities with a rule of life and obtain their inspiration from an older but reinterpreted Monastic tradition. They often live among the poor and marginalised.

The *multiplying stream* "displays considerable continuity with the seeker church and the purpose-driven church movements, though many in this stream define themselves in opposition to their 'parents'." (Richardson 2013:133).

All of these various streams have some resonance amongst groupings in the United Kingdom but there is not a strong or clear set of streams. It might be more accurate to indicate that all of those who are engaging in new mission initiatives are influenced by these various North American writers without replicating the same movements and streams in the UK.

Recent Developments in Germany

Between 2008 and 2012 various books by missional authors were translated into German which initiated the debate, especially Alan Hirsch's and Michael Frost's books.[5] The missional debate in Germany was brought a good step further at confer-

---

[5] To mention are Alan Hirsch's The forgotten ways. Reactivating the missional church (translated in

ences on that topic. To name a few: There are the annual "Studientag Gesell-schaftstransformation" and mbs-Studientage at the *Marburger Bildungs- und Studienzentrum* where Alan Roxburgh, Miroslav Volf, N.T. Wright, Shane Claiborne, Chris How, Johannes Reimer, Tobias Faix were some of the speakers in recent years. The "Forums" of *emergentDeutschland* hosted Brian McLaren, Jason Clark and Alan Roxburgh. Alan Hirsch and Michael Frost spoke at *novavox* and *BFeG-Impulstagung*. Conferences like *Gemeinde 2.0* and *churchconvention* pro-moted the "Fresh expressions of Church" in Germany. Institutions which promote missional topics are the *Studienprogramm Gesellschaftstransformation*, the *Institut für Gemeindeaufbau und Weltmission (IGW)* in Zurich, various *GBFE-Institutes*, and the *Theological Faculty of the University of Greifswald*. A wide range of *articles and books* on missional topics were published by Germans in the last seven years.[6] Outstanding books were recently written by Peter Penner (*Missionale Hermeneutik. Biblische Texte kontextuell und relevant lesen* (2012)), Martin Reppenhagen (*Auf dem Weg zu einer missionalen Kirche: die Diskussion um eine "Missional Church" in den USA* (2011)) and Johannes Reimer (*Die Welt umarmen. Theologie des gesellschaftsrelevanten Gemeindebaus* (2009)).[7] The volumes of the Marburger Transformationsstudien offer a context analysis for local congregations. (Reimer 2012; Faix et al. 2009; Faix/Reimer 2012; Faix/Künkler 2012; Müller et al. 2013) The recent discussion is about the tension or missing clarification between the con-cept of transformation, evangelism and missional (Badenberg/Knödler 2013).

Another debate is about the missional church and the emergent church. Whereas missional describes a theological term, the emergent church is an international movement. It emerged in Germany under the name "Emergent Deutschland" in 2006. The aim of "Emergent Deutschland" is to raise questions of how the gospel is experienced in church and mission within social and cultural change. The partici-pants want to create "safe spaces" which allow an open dialogue on different matters of faith. The international term "Emerging Church" has stirred up much controversy. It is not a new church, what some critics apprehended, but rather a common "emer-gent dialogue". This dialogue is led by a heterogeneous movement (Künkler et al. 2012:38-45; Faix 2014). "Edition Emergent" offers a wide range of topics such as contextualisation, the cultural changes in society, the challenges for the churches, the missional church, the emerging church, spirituality, etc. (Faix/Weißenborn 2007; Faix et al. 2009).

2011), Hirsch's and Michael Frost's books The shaping of the things to come. Innovation and Mis-sion for the 21st-Centry Church (translated in 2008) and ReJesus: A wild Messiah for a Missional Church (translated in 2009). Alan Roxburgh's Missional. Joining God in the Neighborhood (trans-lated in 2012) and The Missional Leader (translated in 2011, co-Authored with Fred Romanuk).

[6] Publishers which publish missional books are Francke-Buch in Marburg, Neufeld-Verlag in Schwarzenfeld.

[7] There are occasional articles in *evangelikale missiologie* (e.g. Kröck 2010, Klassen 2008). The GBFE yearbook of 2009 had the topic Missional Theology (Ebeling/Meier 2009). To mention are also the *12 Thesis for a missional Theology* (2009); the *13 Thesis for a missional Christology* (2011) and the *15 Thesis for a missional Ecclesiology* (2013) of the Zurich based Institut für Gemeindeauf-bau und Weltmission. The bi-annual conference *Mission-net*, which is commissioned by the Europe-an Evangelical Missionary Association (EEMA) and the European Evangelical Alliance (EEA adopted the *Missional Manifesto* (2011) drafted by Ed Stetzer and others.

What we witness in both Europe and North America is a fracturing of the original concerns raised by Lesslie Newbigin. The various streams outlined above represent a diffuse response to the troubled relationship between church and culture. The absence of a dominating figure such as Newbigin has caused a certain loss of direction. With that in mind we turn our attention to the question, how might this lack of focus be approached. Can the missional movement find again a focus and a direction to help the church in its missionary quest to engage with a culture which contains many "post" themes?

The Missional Problem

In many ways the discussion after the publication of *The Missional Church* in 1998 needed to be focussed on the question, what kind of mission would be transformative of both church and culture? That is the question which Newbigin was originally raising and is to a large extent the question that the churches in the West need to find ways of addressing today. In thinking about how that question might be tackled, it is good to remind ourselves that this is not a new problem. In many ways, it represents a problem that emerges whenever the church crosses a significant cultural boundary. In the case of the Western world, mission is not so much entering a new (overseas) world so much as Western culture itself having entered into a divorce from its Christian roots, represents a new and challenging cultural context with which the church must now grapple.

Christianity and Culture – From Jewish Sect to World Faith

At a very early stage in its development Christianity crossed a crucial barrier. It ceased to be a movement within Judaism, where the majority of the followers of a Jewish Messiah were already Jews, worshipping in what were effectively Jesus' or Messianic synagogues, to one where the majority of the participants had never been Jews. The question that the church inevitably had to grapple with was symbolically presented as a battle over circumcision but was in reality addressing the question, is it necessary to be a Jew in order to be a follower of Jesus? Although the answer may be obvious to us, separated as we are by 2,000 years of history, it was clearly not a simple matter then. Interestingly we might pose the question differently now, does a Jew have to become a Gentile in order to be a follower of Jesus and by extension, does someone who is culturally Muslim have to cease to be part of that culture in order to be a follower of Jesus? Framed in that way, we can see that these are not simple questions.

Mission and the Crossing of Cultural Barriers

Once Christianity was freed from the cultural confines of a particular way of expressing what it meant to be a follower of the Messiah, the issue of what the Christian community might look like has remained a challenge whenever Christianity has crossed a particular cultural barrier. Those who first take the message to the new cultural context inevitably bring their own cultural expression of the faith – in the case of European missionaries to Africa and Asia, European architectural styles, complete with pews and pipe organs, and with an accompanying prohibition on drums, clapping and dancing in church. Part of the genius of Christianity has been its ability to express the essential life of the church in an almost limitless variety of cultural forms. At the same time, it necessarily retains the ability to critique the culture that it begins to adopt using the historic tools of the Bible, the ethical tradition that flows from sacred texts and the particular expression of catholicity or global debate which influences local practice.

Bosch and the Concept of Paradigm Shifts in Mission

The South African missiologist David Bosch (1991) borrowed the notion of his paradigm shifts in mission[8] from the work of Hans Küng (1984). In turn, Küng had adopted the concept from the work of Thomas Kuhn (1970) who had initially used the notion of paradigm shifts to describe the way in which science moved from one significant set of ideas to another. Küng could see that the church looked radically different in various cultural settings.[9] As we can see this is a very European way of looking at church history. The story would be told differently in other parts of the world, including that of the Orthodox world, which, although part of Europe, also transcended a purely European context.

Bosch understood that these various forms of church, shaped as they were by their cultural context, also engaged in mission in very different ways. We might even go further and suggest that it was a shift in cultural context that produced something of a crisis for the church. That crisis in turn produced a missiological response of sufficient energy and creativity for the church to be transformed into a differently shaped institution. The new shape of church eventually proved to be more effective in the new cultural milieu in which mission was being conducted. Arguably we are in the middle of just such a crisis now.

The End of Modernity and the Rise of Postmodernity – or Something Else?

The shift in Western culture that has variously been described as the end of modernity or as late modernity has had significant repercussions for institutions of every kind. The underlying process has been a move towards an extreme individuation which has arguably been where the Enlightenment has all along been leading. Secularisation theory concentrates on the impact of this process on institutional religion (or indeed religious belief of any kind) while ignoring the broader impact of the same tendencies for all institutions, political parties, trade unions, the family, and even the Boy Scouts and Girl Guides. As the secularisation story has become discredited it is now possible to speak of a post secular condition to stand alongside all the other "posts" that we are now familiar with – post-industrial, post-colonial, post Christian and postmodern.

Whether we characterize the present situation as postmodern or as simply late modern, we cannot escape the reality that some important shifts have taken place and not

---

[8] Bosch himself never wrote about the missional church. His description of what we understand today under *missional* was the term "the church in mission" (Bosch 1991:368; 378-381; 512).

[9] Küng listed these as: 1) the apocalyptic paradigm of primitive Christianity, 2) the Hellenistic paradigm of the patristic period, 3) the medieval Roman Catholic period, 4) the Protestant (Reformation paradigm), 5) the modern Enlightenment paradigm and 6) the emerging ecumenical paradigm.

all of these are unfriendly towards Christianity. The critique of modernity which turns its own scepticism upon itself – a new hermeneutic of suspicion begins to create a different space for debate. There are many helpful factors in this hermeneutical turn. In this paper there is only space to mention four such elements.

☐ *Secular neutrality is being questioned.* The previous tendency for modernity to gradually end the place of Christianity as making any statement of public truth, suggesting instead that religious statement only had validity as private opinion (and rather worthless superstition for the most part), is being challenged. Modernity's own faith position has been exposed and its place as the sole arbiter of public truth is gradually being dethroned. To be sure, there is a huge pushback against such a challenge but the challenge is real and sustainable.

☐ *Religion is back on the agenda.* Whether secularists like it or not (and they mostly don't), religion is back on the agenda. Whether that is in its unpleasant forms (Al Qaeda and its affiliates) or in more constructive forms, the fact that most of the world is becoming more religious and not less so, religion is not just fading away in the manner that secular thinkers predicted. Europe is no longer seen as the forerunner of things to come – we are not all going to become what Peter Berger called "honorary Swedes" (Berger 1992:32), but rather Europe has become "the exceptional case" the oddity that needs an explanation. That is quite a turnaround in less than a decade! (Berger 2005; Künkler 2009)

☐ *New opportunities for Christianity.* As the State and the Market have continued their centuries-old contest – one marked by both collision and collusion, many have come to value the contribution that faith communities can make to a society under stress. Whether it is the social campaigning to change attitudes towards the environment, or human poverty, or human trafficking or the debt of the Two-Thirds World, or whether it is the ability to mobilise people locally as volunteers in a wide range of social projects, some politicians have come to recognise that the faith communities have a vibrant and indeed essential role to play. The leaders of faith communities are being courted in a new way by politicians and other public figures in ways that have previously been unforeseen. Churches in particular have a new opportunity to change the nature of the conversation that they might have with their neighbours.

☐ *Reflected in some recent statistics.* These subtle but important changes are being reflected in a whole range of statistics that reveal some important shifts. We will comment later on the change in church attendance statistics but other figures suggest that people are not so much less religious as differently religious.

These shifts in the relationship between Christianity and Western culture are not decisive and certainly do not mark a radically new situation. But they do represent the beginnings of an opportunity, one marked by a lessening of hostility and the creation of some space within which the relationship between Christianity and culture might be reconsidered. As we think about how that space might be understood we might consider some "stances" that the church might adopt in its attempt to re-engage culture from a missionary or missional perspective. We might describe this as a piece of "missional mapping".

Missional Mapping

Having discussed the "missional problem" we want to look at how the mission can be transformative for church and culture.

The German Adventist theologian Stefan Höschele developed in his study *The Role of Empirical Study in Systematic Theology* (2009) a typology of the relationship between church and world in recent theological thinking. How do we deal with "the world"?

Church / World Theology	*static*	*dynamic*
static	**Polemics** apologetic model	**Persuasion** conversionist model
dynamic	**Adaption** contextual model	**Interaction** missional model

❑ The first type is the *contextual model* which tries to adopt the New Testament teachings in a particular situation. Like the apostle Paul, contextual theology tries to become a Jew to the Jews and all things to all men (1Cor 9:20-22). This approach has questioned the monopoly of Eurocentric theological thinking. The irony of contextual theology is that because it carries the word contextual the context may not be analysed properly. "Every 'world' is divided into subgroups, parties, factions, which fight over interpretations of reality. Apart from the question of how to communicate the gospel in this context, how can one be sure that one's particular analysis of the world is adequate?" (Höschele 2009:144).

❑ The second approach is the *apologetic model* which views theology as polemics. This approach wants to unmask evil and to question the context, rather than honouring it. It is characterised by a dichotomist's attitude towards men and does not take empirical experience too seriously. Both the contextual and the apologetic model view the world as static, "while the contextual model values its construction of context, apologetic theologizing is done vis-à-vis a world that is construed as dangerous or inimical" (Höschele 2009:145).

❑ The third theological approach is convinced that the world can be changed, because it has to be changed. The *conversionist model* has a strong transformational impetus. Richard Niebuhr's "Christ the transformer of culture" (Niebuhr 1951:190-229) is characteristic of such an approach. Theology is seen as persuasion. We find this kind of approach in many evangelical missionary theologies of the 20th century "a mixture of tenets of both contextual and apologetic approaches with the addition of a dynamic view of empirical reality" (Höschele 2009:147).

❑ The fourth type, Höschele calls the *missional model*. That type views both theology and the world as dynamic. Theology is seen as interaction, as a conversation (Alan Roxburgh). It is not a theology of the classroom but a theology "of the road" (David Bosch) or a theology "on the way" (Van Engen).

The main question here is not whether we can speak of a missional model at all. Many missional theologians would totally disagree. The point is that the missional conversation has a dynamic view of the church and the world and not a static one. Höschele's typology helps us to reflect the prepositions of many of the debates we have on questions like:

❑ How do we see the gospel?

❑ How do we see the world?

❑ How do we see ourselves (the church) in that?

What is God Doing in Our Neighbourhood?

Having a missional imagination means to pay attention to the church's context (Barrett 2006:181) That means, as Martin shows in the appendix, that we are aware of the shifts in Western culture in late modernity, of the Christian responses toward the social and political contexts in the last century, about the mega trends in society and the church. But the key questions about how missional imagination is used are asked by Alan Roxburgh and Scott Boren: "What is God up to in the neighbourhood? And what are the ways we need to change in order to engage the people in our community who no longer consider church a part of their lives?" (Roxburgh/Boren 2009:20). Often missional churches find themselves at the margins of influence but that offers the opportunity to be an alternative community. How does evangelism, what does a missional existence look like in these heterogeneous contexts?

How can we engage in this conversation? Alan Roxburgh argues: Rethink the Gospel, reconsider the context and re-imagine the church.[10] The practical approach of the interaction of text, context and the Christian community are offered by Van Engen (1996:90-101), Reimer (2009:169-288) (with a missiological emphasis), Faix et al.(2012) and Roxburgh (2010) (with a practical focus). Wherever we are, whether in theological education, in office work, in a mission organisation, in youth work, or in congregations, the central question is: How can we be a witness and a sign of God's kingdom in the context in which we find ourselves? What we can see here is that the way in which we are called to re-imagine the church determines very much the following two questions, of how and where we should do it. That means in a relevant way in and for our society; in our social-cultural space. Our life today is determined by five areas in which we operate: Family, place of work, neighbourhood, leisure time, community (Stängle 2011:113-114). The missional conversation addresses all of these areas.

We need the interaction between the text (the gospel of the kingdom) and the context (needs of the people) and the church. In many cases we have to talk of various contexts as the story of Peter shows. Missional thinking and practise aren't just a cognitive endeavour, these are undertaken by people. God has given his church abilities, gifts and knowledge that we must use. Where these three circles meet: God's kingdom, the gifts of the church and the need of the people we discover, we witness communities which are of cultural relevance for our society.

---

[10] Dietrich Werner (1993:6-25) wrote about nearly every aspect we are discussing today 20 years ago.

Focus only on One Area

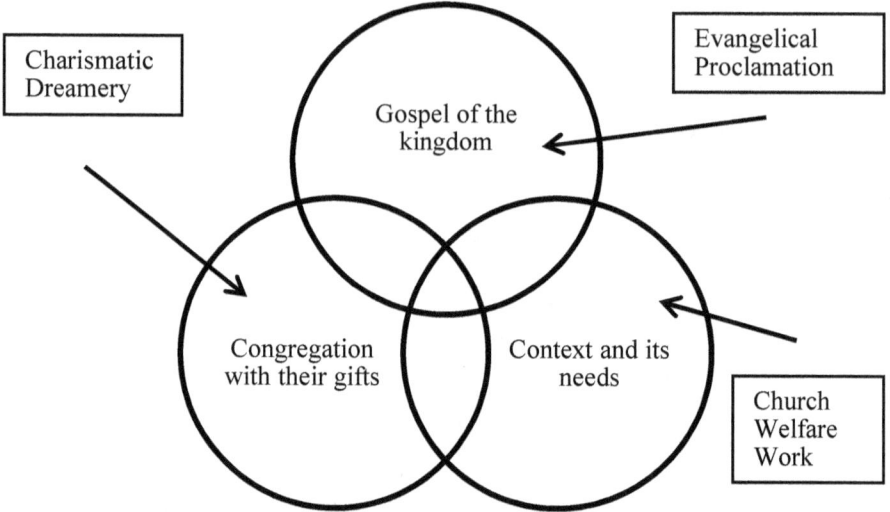

Charismatic
Dreamery

Evangelical
Proclamation

Gospel of the
kingdom

Congregation
with their gifts

Context and its
needs

Church
Welfare
Work

Focus only on Two Areas

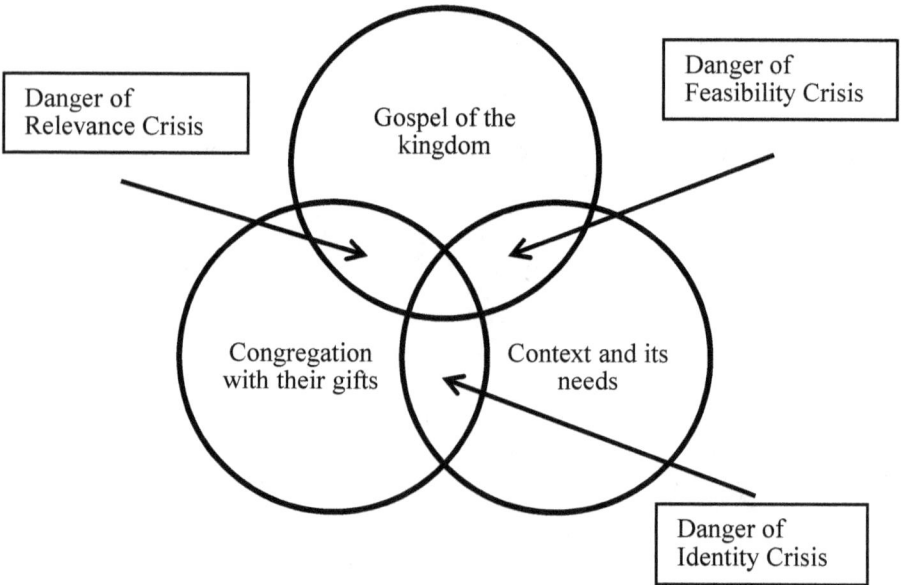

Danger of
Relevance Crisis

Danger of
Feasibility Crisis

Gospel of the
kingdom

Congregation
with their gifts

Context and its
needs

Danger of
Identity Crisis

Missional Conversation

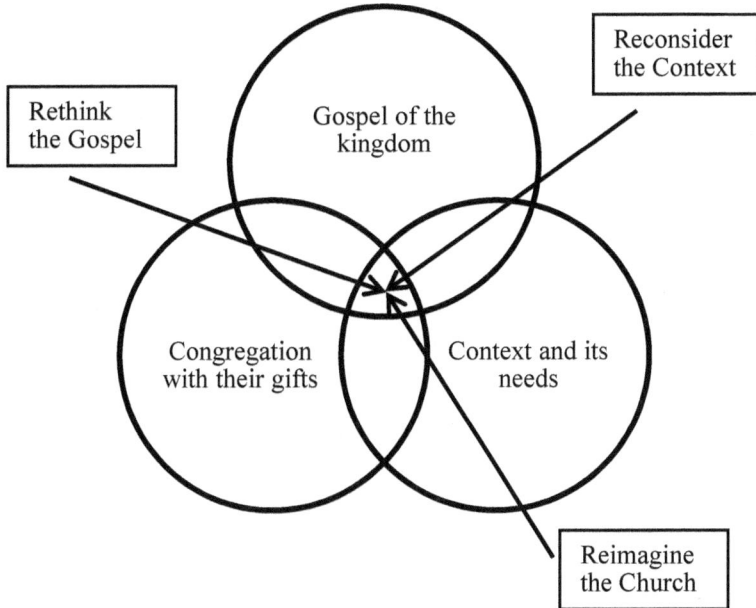

Take Hans' and Peter's situation again. What happens when there is no missional conversation, and they are just looking at one aspect? If one is only *oriented on the gifts*, he will end up in what we call "charismatic dreamery". We have seen many people over the years who know everything about their spiritual gifts and whose focus was only on their gifting and the question of how their gifts can promote their self-efficacy or self-fulfilment. But unless there is a clear focus on the word of God and the context in which people live in, one won't really have an impact on the people around and the community as a whole. If one is only *task-oriented*, one will stress evangelical proclamation. The motto is "Preach the word (...) in season and out of season" (2Tim 4:2). It is disillusioning when one thinks about the outcome. Germany is a country with a long tradition of over 500 years of preaching but rarely with discipleship. The outcome has been empty churches and a shrinking Christendom without power in the last decades. If one is only context-oriented they will end up in a church social work. Again, Germany is a brilliant example. The churches built up a wonderful social work. Today the churches with their charity, the Catholic "Caritas" and the Protestant "Diakonie" are the largest non-governmental employer in this country. However, there is usually little contact between the social work and the local congregation. There are definite dangers and failings when we just focus on one area.

So what would happen if we were to focus on two areas and leave one out? What will be the outcome then? The evangelical context-oriented persons who leave out the gifts of the spirit face a crisis of feasibility. The individual or the team will soon be overwhelmed by the things that need to be done if they do not know what gifts God has endowed them with. The gift- and context-oriented persons will soon find themselves in an identity crisis, because the direction from God's word does not play a practical role in their life. And finally: The only gift- and task-oriented persons will face a crisis of relevance because the context might be quite different from the lifestyle and approach of the congregation.[11]

So how might we move forward to discover a missional church that takes seriously its context, the Word of God and the spiritual gifts given by God? We propose that what is required is a new creative space in which we might act and think. The ingredients of action and reflection are both essential. How might that space be created? As we enter into creative action and careful theological reflection, we will hopefully witness changes in the way we exercise our common life as the church and as practical theologians. Missional is therefore also used to signal a change in how we see the church and how we do theology. Craig Van Gelder proposes a short but helpful explanation of what is meant when one talks about missional:

❑ "God is a missionary God who sends the church into the world. (...)

❑ God's mission in the world is related to the reign (kingdom) of God. (...)

❑ The missional church in an incarnational ministry sent to engage a postmodern, post-Christendom globalized context. (...)

❑ The internal life of the missional church focuses on every believer living as a disciple engaging in mission" (Van Gelder/Zscheile 2010:4).

Propositions

We want to suggest five propositions or elements of a missional agenda that need to be noted and acted upon. These five Propositions are:

❑ Hope lies in our ability to harness the energy of the Roman Catholic Church, the Historic Protestant Churches and the newer Pentecostal and Charismatic Churches. The competitive landscape of Christendom with its mutual hostility between denominations and its misuse of power and influence is still not completely a thing of the past. The old suspicions, hurts, and envy, often well-grounded in actual experience still prevent full hearted cooperation in mission.

❑ *We need to create a conversation with local communities.* Many existing congregations have forgotten how to relate to their surrounding community. In extreme cases they may even blame the community for the decline of the church.

❑ *The energy and creativity of the ethnic church needs to be utilised.* The arrival of many enthusiastic Christians from other lands can be viewed as an encouraging act of God. However, these Christians are not easily integrated into that which already exists and often form their own hermetically sealed congregations. The stated desire of many such congregations is to reach out to all the cit-

---

[11] Jürgen Moltmann addressed the identity crises and the relevance crises already in *The crucified God* in 1972. (Moltmann 1972:12-30).

izens of the land in which they find themselves but the practical realities are very different.

❏ *Church planting will be important for every denomination.* Accepting that some denominations have difficulty with the language of church planting and may feel more comfortable with talk of Fresh Expressions or of Christian communities, it is still the case that denominations or network of churches need to experiment with mission in the form of new congregations or church plants. In part that is because the existing forms of church will simply not allow missional experiment and so new forms of church will sometimes have to grow in parallel with that which already exists.

It is also true that some churches close. There may be good reasons and not such good reasons why this takes place. But provided that new, healthy and vibrant congregations arise to take their place, this need not be a tragedy so much as part of a natural life cycle within a healthy group of congregations.

❏ *We need a Europe-wide conversation between thinking practitioners and practical thinkers.* The last several decades have been marked by many initiatives, many of them coming from the United States, which have been well intentioned, and sometimes well resourced, but arguably have not been well thought through.

One example among many would be that of the DAWN movement. In essence this attempt to encourage saturation church planting across Europe was imported from its original context in the Philippines, mediated through the USA and translated into a number of national contexts in Europe with little or no thought given to any contextualisation of the missiological assumptions that lay behind the initiative. We can also see that there have been many profound missiological and theological declarations which have occupied much time, creative thought and effort but which have not connected with those who might actually use these insights to make a difference on the ground. The missional church will be of little use if it is only a theological construct. The answer to our situation will never be solely another book.

Creating a Missional People

As we have indicated already, the Missional Church has sometimes wrongly been seen as yet another "model" of church to be set alongside "the emerging church", or "seeker sensitive churches" or "the new Calvinism". That would be a fundamental misunderstanding of the nature of the missional conversation. There is not enough space in this paper to review the contours and varieties of that conversation but a starting point would be to describe the missional conversation as an orientation towards mission.

Four key orientations are commonly noted. These are not unique or necessarily original or profound, but taken together they denote a creative stance that produces a certain quality of missional life. Missional churches are shaped by practices which "include baptism, the Lord's Supper, forgiveness, accountability, hospitality, prayer, watching over one another in love, how the church deals with conflict, and how it makes decisions" (Barrett 2006:180).

❑ *Called*: The Missional Church understands that its fundamental reason for being surrounds a calling to the world. Mission is the *raison d'etre* for the church. The church never exists for its own sake.

❑ *Gathered*: The art of gathering people so that they become a community and not just an audience requires significant skill, dedication and effort. A missional church is profoundly a missional community and not a passive group of followers or – worse still – listeners of the word but not doers of the word.

❑ *Connected*: Missional congregations do not exist in isolation from other congregations and from their own inheritance and tradition. They are connected to the past and to the saints in other places. We might call this a missional catholicity. The 'catholicity question' is one that faces many congregations today. Congregations need to know both that they are connected and how they are connected to the whole body of Christ.

❑ *Sent:* It would be all too easy for a church that has discovered a significant community life, was aware of its identity and was comfortable with its understanding of its own tradition and inheritance, to become all too centred in its own life. A missional church will take creative risks with its own life in order to be in the world, serving its neighbourhood but also seeking the lost.

Appendix:
The Changing Missiological Landscape –
a British View, by Martin Robinson

Christian Reactions to the Changing Shape of Europe

The comments made above and the text to follow does not describe the whole of the West or indeed the whole of Europe. We need to recognise that there are at least four Europes as far as faith and indeed many other social trends are concerned. These are: a) The Protestant North; b) the Catholic South; c) the Orthodox East and d) the South East of Europe (largely the Balkan states) with their very mixed populations in terms of religion and ethnicity. The descriptors that I am using in this paper belong almost entirely to the first of these categories. With that in mind, we can characterise the significant periods over the last 100 years as follows:

❑ *Christendom is broken and needs to be mended 1918-1945*. The period between the two World Wars was characterised, as we have already mentioned, by a sense that Christendom had become fractured. Christian leaders attempted in a whole variety of ways – different in different nations, to attempt to reassert the influence of the church by demonstrating the relevance of Christianity to the social and political context in which they found themselves. The churches and their leaders could still think in terms of their national influence and still attempt to describe their nations as constituting a Christian culture of some kind.

❑ *1950's – we can fix it*. During the 1950's most nations in the west experienced a growth in church attendance and membership. Significant building programmes responded to changes in the distribution of the population, in particular the growing suburbanisation of the west. Evangelists such as Billy Graham and Oral Roberts, to name but two, offered very visible examples of the re-building of faith and commitment through crusades and campaigns of various kinds.

That kind of growth helped to develop the recovery of evangelical and pente-costal expressions of Christianity. An evangelical renaissance dates from this period as well as a growing accommodation between evangelical and pentecos-tal leaders. Pentecostals were beginning to join the evangelical mainstream. It really did look to many church leaders as if the early fracturing of Christendom had been accomplished.

❑ *1960's – disconnect.* The period referred to by sociologists as the "long 1960's" dating from 1965 to around 1971, then revealed in starkest form that far from Christendom being mended, it was in reality irreparably broken. Many denom-inations in the north of Europe saw their attendances half in a single decade. Writers such as Callum Brown claim that a new era had arrived when for the first time in centuries the faith ceased to be transmitted within families. The sense that a new secular age had arrived was evident. In this new framework of reference, religion was now marginalised as a preparation for irrelevance and subsequent extinction. The Church and western culture would no longer be in-timately connected but would go their separate ways.

❑ *1970's to 2000 – is it possible for the church to grow in Europe at all?* The shock engendered by this sudden drop in adherence and relevance caused the churches to question whether they could survive in any form. This was a period characterised by a shift towards a new evangelical, Pentecostal and charismatic mainstream (the EPC shift), and a search for methods, programmes, and move-ments that would help the church to survive in the midst of this new crisis.

Often these new programmes would come to Europe and other parts of the west from the United States. Even though church in that land was also impacted by the same societal forces as those present in Europe, for the most part, the churches in the USA still retained a degree of entrepreneurial vigour which had been lost in other parts of the western church. Suspicion and fascination were possibly present in equal measure when European church leaders visited the various expressions of Christianity in the USA.

By the close of the 20th century, the churches of Europe were beginning to an-swer the question about their survival with a cautious and conditional "yes we can survive." The caution recognised that the church could only survive as a minority group in a plural religious scene. The conditional dimension recog-nised that it was churches with a stronger EPC dimension that were more likely to survive.

❑ *21st century – the missional question.* By the beginning of the 21st century some, albeit a minority, Christian leaders had the courage to ask a different kind of question than simply the survival question. To some extent their new found ambition was influenced by encounters with Newbigin and the *Gospel and Our Culture movement.* They began to ask, can we reconnect with culture and imagination in terms of people movements? What would it look like to see Europe as a mission field and equip ourselves accordingly? What would mis-sion to this culture consist of? These were very different kinds of questions than those concerned with church growth and church health. Of course it often takes healthy and growing churches to ask those questions and certainly one might expect churches with that kind of missionary concern to grow and be healthy. But the central focus of a missionary agenda is very different than a concern about the survival of the church.

Societal Mega Trends in Europe

❑ *The Secularisation of Europe.* It is increasingly clear that the secularisation thesis is deeply flawed and even though we are in some sense in a post Christendom situation that reality cannot adequately be interpreted through the simple lens of secularisation. As some authors have suggested, Europe is not so much less religious as differently religious. Others have spoken of the re-sacralisation of Europe and the extent to which the west is recovering a sense of the spiritual as distinct from the religious. That distinction would not have made sense in an early age and it is possible that as religious institutions change their shape, it may not be a distinction that will hold in the future.

❑ *God is Back.* The book with the title *God is Back: How the Global Revival of Faith is Changing the World*, written by the editor-in-chief of *The Economist*, John Micklethwait (2009) with writing partner Adrian Wooldridge, makes it clear that Europe is the "exceptional case" that needs explanation and can no longer think of itself as the forerunner of the destiny of the rest of the world. Indeed as Woolridge and Micklethwait assert, if Europe is to communicate effectively with the rest of the world, Europeans need to reassess the impact of religion in a more positive light than has been the tendency in recent decades.

❑ *The rest of the world arrives in Europe.* In part that necessary re-evaluation is driven by the arrival of significant numbers of migrants from the rest of the world. Not only are the various world religions now occupying public space in Europe, but the centres of all of the major cities of Western Europe are increasingly influenced by large numbers of Christians from other continents. These newly arrived Christians are populating congregations in the historic denominations as well as creating a large variety of new denominations, primarily of a pentecostal and neo-pentecostal character. One such denomination, the *Redeemed Christian Church of God,* claims to have more than 700 congregations in the UK with a membership in excess of 80.000. That makes them the arguably the fourth largest denomination in the UK, something that has arisen within a mere 20 years.

Church Mega Trends

❑ *The huge declines in European church attendance have slowed or halted.* There is increasing evidence that at least in Northern Europe the huge declines of the recent past are either slowing or in some exceptional cases have now ended. The situation of England, with its greater resource amongst the evangelical community and with the significant impact of around 1 million new Christian migrants, is possibly further advanced than other European nations but there are grounds for thinking that just such a shift may be beginning in other nations too.

❑ *The shape of the church is changing.* Part of the reason for this shift is that local church life is beginning to demonstrate a new creativity in worship, in experimenting with new forms of the church, in spiritual vigour and in a local connectedness with the communities that congregations seek to serve. The movement *Fresh Expressions* (Cray 2004) which began in the *Anglican Church* has spread to a number of other denominations within England and is increasingly impacting other northern European nations.

❑ *Nominal Christianity is departing in favour of faith.* In a post Christendom situation where there is no longer any social advantage in belonging to a church, the reason for making an active choice to belong have more to do with personal faith and commitment and less to do with inherited tradition. Under these circumstances, the spiritual, practical and financial resources of the church are potentially strengthened.

❑ *The mainstream of the church is shifting.* A corollary of the shift in commitment, towards that of personal choice and the language of conversion, is that the mainstream of the church looks very different both in terms of theology and in terms of actual denominational life. We have already commented on the growth of the EPC segment in church life and that growth is reflected in the growth of the newer denominations alongside the shrinking of the older denominations. In the UK, the *United Reformed Church* numbered some 250.000 members at its inception in 1971. At that time, the *Assemblies of God* numbered some 25.000 members. Today the Assemblies of God have probably become largely than the United Reformed Church, which presently numbers less than 90.000 members. In short, we now have to redefine what constitutes the mainstream.

❑ *Church often (not always) looks different.* One result of the shift in the mainstream of the church is that church life locally begins to look different. That difference is manifest in a whole variety of traits, ranging from the use of small groups, the attempt to develop lay leadership, an increasing tendency towards team approaches in ministry, contemporary worship styles, and attempts to think about the accessibility of church life for those who are coming for the first time.

❑ *Spirituality is on the agenda.* The last several decades have seen the growth of a whole range of activities, which broadly indicate a new interest in spiritual depth. Spiritual direction, the growth in popularity of retreat centres, the publication of books on the inner spiritual life, the attraction of places such as Taizé, the recovery of pilgrimage. See the contribution of Frère Richard in this volume. These are all indicators that there is a significant renewal of spiritual life amongst many Christians who are seeking to take the life of faith more seriously.

❑ *A great deal is happening in terms of activity and initiatives.* The growth of activity in the spiritual realm has been accompanied by a new desire to serve local communities in practical ways. This can be described as the move back to the neighbourhood, and is accompanied by a growth in the practice of what has become known as "local theology". Alongside that attempt at community exegesis has come the development of what some are calling "a theology of place".

All of these tendencies, trends or movements are encouraging. They are by no means universal and they vary in intensity and vibrancy in different nations across Europe. But sharp eyed observers can detect enough of these contours to suggest that the church is no longer deep in shock. It has begun the process of hopeful recovery even if that is from a position of exile, no longer leading society but witnessing from the margins of our culture. These hopeful signs need to be strengthened and encouraged by an active missional theology and practice.

Literature

Badenberg, Robert/Knödler, Friedemann (ed.). 2013. *Evangelisation und Transformation. „Zwei Münzen oder eine Münze mit zwei Seiten?"* Referate der Jahrestagung des Arbeitskreises für evangelikale Missiologie (AfeM). Nürnberg/Bonn: VTR/VKW.

Barth, Karl. 1957. *Die Theologie und die Mission.* Vortrag gehalten an der brandenburgischen Missionskonferenz in Berlin am 11. April 1932, in: idem 1957. Theologische Fragen und Antworten. Gesammelte Vorträge / 3. Band. Zollikon: Evangelischer Verlag, 100-126.

Barrett, David. 2006. Defining the Missional Church, in: Krabill, James R./ Sawatzky, Walter/ Van Engen, Charles (ed.). 2006. *Evangelical, Ecumenical and Anabaptist Missiologies in Conversation.* Essays in Honor of Wilbert Shenk. Maryknoll: Orbis, 177-183.

Berger, Peter L. 1992. *A far glory: The quest for faith in an age of credulity.* New York: The Free Press.

Berger, Peter L. 2005. The desecularisation of the world: a global overview, in: idem (ed.). 2005. *The desecularisation of the world: resurgent religion and world politics.* Washington DC: Ethics and Public Policy Centre, 1-18.

Billings, Todd. 2008. What makes a church missional? Freedom from cultural captivity does not mean freedom from tradition, in: *Christianity Today*, March 2008, 56-59.

Bosch, David. 1991. *Transforming Mission. Paradigm Shifts in Theology of Mission.* Maryknoll/New York: Orbis Books. [Transl.: 2012. *Mission im Wandel. Paradigmenwechsel in der Missionstheologie.* Mit einem neuen abschließenden Kapitel von Darell I. Guder und Martin Reppenhagen. Giessen/Basel: Brunnen].

Cray, Graham (ed.). 2004. *Mission-shaped-Church. Church Planting and Fresh Expressions of Church in an Changing Context.* London: Church House Publishing. [Transl.: Herbst, Michael (ed.). 2006. *Mission bringt Gemeinde in Form. Gemeindepflanzung und neue Ausdrucksformen gemeindliches Lebens in einem sich wandelnden Kontext.* Neukirchen-Vluyn: Aussaat].

Doornenbal, Robert. 2012. *Crossroads. An Exploration of the Emerging-Missional Conversation with a Special Focus on 'Missional Leadership' and its Challenges for Theological Education.* Delft: Eburon Academic Publisher.

Ebeling, Rainer/Meier, Alfred (ed.). 2009. *Missionale Theologie.* GBFE Jahrbuch 2009. Marburg: Francke.

Faix, Tobias/Weißenborn, Thomas (ed.). 2007. *Zeitgeist. Kultur und Evangelium in der Postmoderne.* Marburg: Verlag der Franke-Buchhandlung.

Faix, Tobias/Weißenborn, Thomas/Aschoff, Peter (ed.). 2009. *Zeitgeist 2. Postmoderne Heimatkunde.* Marburg: Verlag der Franke-Buchhandlung.

Faix, Tobias/Reimer, Johannes/Brecht, Volker (ed.). 2009. *Die Welt verändern. Grundfragen einer Theologie der Transformation.* Transformationsstudien Bd. 2. Marburg: Francke.

Faix, Tobias/Reimer, Johannes (ed.). 2012. *Die Welt verstehen. Kontextanalyse als Sehhilfe für die Gemeinde.* Transformationsstudien Bd. 3. Marburg: Francke.

Faix, Tobias/ Künkler, Tobias (ed.). 2012. *Die verändernde Kraft des Evangeliums.* Transformationsstudien. Bd. 4. Marburg: Francke.

Faix, Tobias. 2014. Mission und Evangelisation, in: Kunz, Ralph / Schlag, Thomas (ed.). 2014. *Handbuch für Kirchen- und Gemeindeentwicklung.* Neukirchen: Vylun: Neukirchner Verlag.

Frost, Michael/Hirsch, Alan. 2003. The Shaping of Things to Come: Innovation and Mission for the 21st-century Church. Peabody/Mass: Hendrickson. [Transl.: Frost, Michael/Hirsch, Alan. 2008. *Die Zukunft gestalten. Innovation und Evangelisation in der Kirche des 21. Jahrhunderts.* Glashütten: C&P).

Guder, Darrell (ed.). 1998. *Missional Church: A Vision for the Sending of the Church in North America.* Grand Rapids: Eerdmans.

Hartenstein, Karl. 1952. Theologische Besinnung, in: Freytag, Walter (ed.). 1952. *Mission zwischen gestern und morgen.* Vom Gestaltwandel der Weltmission der Christenheit im Licht der Konferenz des Internationalen Missionsrats in Willingen, Stuttgart: Ev. Missionsverlag.

Hirsch, Alan/Frost, Michael. 2009. *ReJesus: A wild Messiah for a Missional Church.* Peabody/Mass.: Hendrickson Publishers [Transl.: Hirsch, Alan/Frost Michael. 2009. *Der wilde Messias: Mission und Kirche von Jesus neu gestaltet.* Schwarzenfeld: Neufeld.]

Hirsch, Alan. 2006. *The forgotten ways. Reactivating the missional church.* Grand Rapids: Brazos Press [Transl.: Hirsch, Alan. 2011. *Vergessene Wege: Die Wiederentdeckung der missionalen Kraft der Kirche.* Schwarzenfeld: Neufeld].

Höschele, Stefan. 2009. Sola Experientia Facit Theologum? The Role of Empirical Study in Systematic Theology, in: *Spes Christiana 20*, 141-152.

Institut für Weltmission und Gemeindeaufbau (Hg.). 2009. *12 Thesen für eine missionale Theologie,* in: http://blog.igw.edu/2009/03/10/12-thesen-zur-missionalen-theologie/ (27.09.2014).

Institut für Weltmission und Gemeindeaufbau (Hg.). 2011. *13 Thesen für eine missionale Christologie,* in: http://www.igw.edu/assets/data/Publikationen/ 13_Thesen_Missionale_Christologie_Web.pdf (27.09.2014).

Institut für Weltmission und Gemeindeaufbau (Hg.). 2013. *15 Thesen für eine missionale Ekklesiologie,* in: http://www.igw.edu/assets/data/Publikationen/Thesen-Ekklesiologie-D1-Web.pdf (27.09.2014).

Klassen, Harold. 2008. *Dritte Welle moderner christlicher Schulen: Plädoyer für eine missionales Schulmodell,* in: em 2-2008, 51-55.

Kröck, Thomas. 2010. *Missionale Ekklesiologie und ganzheitlicher Dienst:* Bericht vom Workshop „Missional ecclesiology meets Holistic ministry" der CCD Konferenz 2010, in: em 3-2010, 137-141.

Küng, Hans 1984. Was meint Paradigmenwechsel?, in: ders./Tracy, David (ed.). 1984. *Theologie – wohin? Auf dem Weg zu einem neuen Paradigma.* Zürich/Köln: Benziger Verlag, 19-26.

Künkler, Tobias/ Faix, Tobias/ Bachmann, Arne. 2012. *Emerging Church verstehen. Eine Einladung zum Dialog.* Einfach emergent Band 1. Marburg: Verlag der Francke-Buchhandlung.

Künkler, Tobias. 2009. Fremde Heimat?! Eine Wiederentdeckung des christlichen Abendlandes für die Kommunikation des Evangeliums, in: Faix, Tobias/Weißenborn, Thomas/Aschoff, Peter (ed.). 2009. *Zeitgeist 2. Postmoderne Heimatkunde.* Marburg: Verlag der Franke-Buchhandlung, 18-26.

Kuhn, Thomas. 1970. *The Structure of Scientific Revolutions.* 2nd Edition. Chicago: The University of Chicago Press. [Transl.: Kuhn, Thomas. 1973. *Die Struktur wissenschaftlicher Revolutionen.* Frankfurt a. M.: Suhrkamp].

Stetzer, Ed/Hirsch Alan et al. 2011. *Missional Manifesto,* in: http://www.edstetzer.com/missional-manifesto/ (27.09.2014)

Micklethwait, John/Wooldridge, Arian. 2009. *God is Back: How the Global Revival of Faith is Changing the World.* New York: Penguin Press.

Moltmann, Jürgen. 1972. *Der gekreuzigte Gott. Das Kreuz Christi als Grund und Kritik christlicher Theologie.* München: Chr. Kaiser. [Engl.: Moltmann, Jürgen. 1973. *The Crucified God: The Cross of Christ As the Foundation and Criticism of Christian Theology,* London: SCM Press].

Newbigin, Lesslie. 1983. *The Other Side of 1984. Question for the Churches,* Geneva: World Council of Churches. [Transl.: Newbigin, Lesslie. 1985. Salz der Erde?! Fragen an die Kirchen heute. Neukirchen-Vluyn: Schriftenmissions-Verlag].

Newbigin, Lesslie. 1986. *Foolishness to the Greeks.* Grand Rapids: Eerdmans. [Transl.: Newbigin, Lesslie. 1989. *"Den Griechen eine Torheit". Das Evangelium und unsere westliche Kultur.* Neukirchen-Vluyn: Aussaat Verlag].

Niebuhr, H. Richard. 1951. *Christ and Culture.* New York: Harper & Row.

Parzany, Ulrich. 2013. Wir werden missional – und streichen evangelistische Dienste!?, in: Badenberg, Robert/ Knödler, Friedemann (ed.). 2013. *Evangelisation und Transformation. „Zwei Münzen oder eine Münze mit zwei Seiten?"* Referate der Jahrestagung des Arbeitskreises für evangelikale Missiologie (AfeM). Nürnberg/Bonn: VTR/VKW, 17-18.

Penner, Peter F. 2012. *Missionale Hermeneutik. Biblische Texte kontextuelle und relevant lesen.* Schwarzenfeld: Neufeld.

Reimer, Johannes. 2009. *Die Welt umarmen. Theologie des gesellschaftsrelevanten Gemeindebaus.* Transformationsstudien Band 1. Marburg: Verlag der Francke Buchhandlung.

Reimer, Johannes. 2012. Der Missionale Aufbruch. Paradigmenwechsel im Gemeindedenken, in: Faix, Tobias/ Künkler, Tobias (ed.). 2012. *Die verändernde Kraft des Evangeliums.* Transformationsstudien. Bd. 4. Marburg: Francke, 303-328.

Reppenhagen, Martin. 2011. *Auf dem Weg zu einer missionalen Kirche. Die Diskussion um eine „Missional Church" in den USA.* Neukirchen-Vluyn: Neukirchner Verlag.

Richardson, Rick. 2013. Emerging Missional Movements: an Overview and Assessment of Some Implications for Mission(s), in: *International Bulletin of Missionary Research 37*, No 3, 131-136.

Roxburgh, Alan J. 2010. *Missional Map-making. Skills for Leading in Times of Transition.* San Francisco: Jossey-Bass.

Roxburgh, Alan J. / Boren, M. Scott. 2009. *Introducing the Missional Church. What it is, Why it Matters, How to Become One?*, Grand Rapids; Bakers.

Roxburgh, Alan/Romanuk, Fred. 2006. *The Missional Leader: Equipping your Church to reach a Changing World.* San Francisco: Jossey-Bass (dt. 2011. *Missionale Leiterschaft. Gemeinde bauen in einer sich verändernden Welt.* Marburg: Francke.)

Roxburgh, Alan 2011. *Missional. Joining God in the Neighborhood.* Grand Rapids: Baker Books (dt. 2012. *Missional. Mit Gott in der Nachbarschaft leben.* Marburg: Francke.

Van Engen, Charles. 1996. *Mission on the Way: Issues in Mission Theology.* Grand Rapids: Baker.

Van Gelder, Craig/Zscheile, Dwight J. 2010. *The Missional Church in Perspective: Mapping Trends and Shaping the Conversation.* Grand Rapids: Baker Academic.

Werner, Dietrich. 1993. Missio Dei in unserem Land. Ökumenische Gemeindeerneuerung, in: *Zeitschrift für Mission 19*, Heft 1, 6-25.

Frère Richard

The Missional Life of the Taizé Community:
Experiences and Theological Reflections

Let me start by telling you how it is that I am here with you this morning. A story can help to understand things better, easier and sometimes deeper. I can of course not tell the whole story of why I am here. This would include also my life story. You can hear from my accent that I come from Switzerland. But immediately after graduating from high school I went to Taizé in France. There I have spent most of my life. Concerning my childhood and youth, I would only say that participating in this Congress here at Offenburg recalls some memories. "Allianzveranstaltungen", as events organized by the Evangelical Alliance were called, belong to my childhood memories.

The more recent part of the story why I am here this morning starts in 2010. At that time, we, the Taizé Community, were planning a European Young Adults Meeting in Berlin. It was to take place from 28 December 2011 to 1 January 2012 in the German capital. We were invited by the churches, especially the ÖRBB, the Ecumenical Council of Berlin-Brandenburg.

During the preparations, we learned from the administration of the Berlin exhibition halls that Mission-Net planned a congress in Berlin for the same date. We contacted Evi Rodemann. We would have got the exhibition halls anyway, since we had asked for them first. But we wanted to talk, because it is a particular concern of the annual European Young Adults Meetings to involve, if possible, all the local Christians of a city and its surrounding for the welcome of the young people coming from all over Europe. We would have been sorry if two large Christian events took place simultaneously in the same city. The Berliners are accustomed to diversity in all respects. Neither do different sorts of Christians disturb them. Yet we hoped that a common witness would speak more clearly than parallel events, which outsiders could interpret as a Christian incapacity of being and working together.

The Mission-Net Congress then took place in Erfurt. This could have been the end of the story. But it was not. During the preparations for the European Meeting in Strasbourg and in the surrounding places in Alsace and in Ortenau, we learned from parishes in Offenburg that the Mission-Net Congress would take place at exactly the same time here in Offenburg! I must say that we were quite surprised. The probability that, two years after Berlin, the two events would happen to take place in the same place again was extremely low. An unfortunate coincidence? We were also worried: would this mean for some churches and Christians in Offenburg to have to choose one or the other? And above all: what about the common Christian witness?

Brother George and I contacted Evi Rodemann again. It turned out that the Kirchentag in Hamburg would be a good opportunity to meet. So, on a sunny May afternoon we had coffee together on the pier of Hamburg and got to know each other. We talked about this and that, youth and the church, the meetings in Taizé, about songs and praying together, and also about the question whether the two events, the Mission-Net Congress and the European meeting, could not overlap somehow. So they would not be an unfortunate competition, but a piece of a common journey and common witness. The idea came up that one of us brothers from Taizé would participate in Offenburg, and participants of the Mission-Net congress could join a common prayer and a workshop in Strasbourg. That is why I am here this morning.

I have told this story in such detail because, in my opinion, it points to a very central aspect of missional life. In the high priestly prayer Jesus prayed, "May they all be one so that the world may believe that you have sent me" (Jn 17:21). Whether we as Christians today are able to continue the mission which Jesus brought into the world and people can come to faith through our witness, depends decisively on whether we are one in Christ's love or not. Therefore, in Taizé, the reconciliation among Christians has priority. And that is why, when we are invited to organize a meeting like now in Strasbourg, in Alsace and in Ortenau, we begin by contacting the various local churches in order to pray and work together.

In the following, I first want to speak about Taizé, its history and the meetings that take place throughout the whole year, year after year. And then, in a second part, add some biblical-theological considerations.

The Story of Taizé

Taizé is the name of a small village in Burgundy. It is an old village with a small church, dating from the 12th century. The history of our community begins eight hundred years later. In 1940, the young man Roger Schutz, who later became known under the name of Brother Roger, came to Taizé. He was born in Switzerland in 1915. His childhood and youth were in a time of war and peace. The year of his birth, 1915, was the second year of the First World War, the year of his arrival in Taizé, 1940, the second year of the Second World War.

In the first years in Taizé, from 1940 to 1942, Brother Roger helped refugees, especially Jews, to continue their way further south or to Switzerland. The demarcation line, which separated the occupied part of France from the so-called "zone libre", the unoccupied zone in the southeast, passed not very far north of Taizé. When, in 1942, all of France was occupied, Brother Roger was denounced and could escape the Gestapo just in time. He left Taizé and returned to Geneva. As soon as it was possible, in winter 1944/45, he came back to Taizé, this time with the first future brothers. The young men prayed together, managed the farm and welcomed, at the request of a juvenile judge, children first in a house in the neighbouring village and then directly in Taizé.

The fact that Taizé started in the time of the Second World War is not only a chronological coincidence. Brother Roger told us often the story of his maternal grandmother. She had experienced the First World War in northern France. From her, little Roger inherited the question how it is that Christians so easily speak of love and yet have been fighting so many wars and still do. He realized that the divisions among Christians belie the gospel.

"His *disciples* would have to *look more* redeemed!" said Nietzsche about the Christians, „for me to learn to have faith in *their Redeemer*." Brother Roger certainly agreed. But it is as if he had added: "They would have to love each other more fully from the heart for people to learn to believe." But he did not want to write books and give lectures about the unity of the Church. Instead, he heard the call to follow Jesus in a simple common life. In 1953, he wrote a rule for the brothers who, starting with Easter 1949, had committed themselves to a common life in the ancient monastic tradition. It contains these lines: "Never resign yourself to the scandal of the separation of Christians, all so readily professing love for their neighbour, yet remaining divided. Make the unity of Christ's Body your passionate concern."

The Taizé Community could have remained small and hidden. It remained small, even today we are not even a hundred brothers, of whom about twenty live in groups of two to six on other continents. It did not remain hidden. Countless people have now visited Taizé; many have come to or rediscovered faith in Taizé. What started in Taizé radiates far beyond Taizé. This can probably not be explained, but perhaps understood in the light of the Gospel. Jesus said: "Nothing is hidden that will not be known" (Mt 10:26). He also spoke of the mustard seed that grows into a big tree.

The word "parable" is a keyword for Taizé. Often Brother Roger said and wrote that we want to live as "a parable of community", or even a "parable of reconciliation". Instead of "parable", you may say "sign". Since 1949, every brother who makes his life commitment in our Community is told: "The Lord Christ, in his compassion and his love for you, has chosen you to be in the Church a sign of brotherly love. He calls you to live out, with your brothers, the parable of community."

Signs and parables speak. Maybe you do not understand them right away – many people did not understand the parables of Jesus, not even the disciples understood them at once. But who starts to understand, discovers in them more and more even what is hidden, "mysteries of the kingdom of God" (Lk 8:10), as Jesus says in the context of the parables.

It seems to me that something like this has happened in Taizé. People, especially many young people, have understood the sign of brotherly love and the parable of the common life. By the late fifties, more visitors came to Taizé. And in the sixties and seventies, the youth meetings developed and brought to this day thousands of people to Taizé.

The Backbone of the youth meetings are the daily common prayers. Three times a day the bells ring, and everything stops, the work, the conversations, the welcoming. It is impressive to observe how ordinary young people move to the church in hundreds and sometimes thousands. They often come even before the bells ring.

At every common prayer, a passage from the Bible is read aloud in several languages. This is followed by a song and about ten minutes of silence. At the beginning, this silence is unusual for most of our guests. But after a few days, they tell us how much it means to them. I think the common silence is possible for the following reasons. The brothers are present and pray, whether people come or not. The church is a warm and welcoming place, there is the light of candles and icons, and you can sit on the floor like at home. There is the beauty of the singing. If young people tell us sometimes that Taizé is a second home for them, this has mainly to do, I believe, with the fact that they make in the church the experience of being at home with God.

During the week they spend in Taizé, every morning the guests meet in age groups. A brother gives an introduction to the Bible text of the day, shows links to the present-day world, and gives questions for the subsequent discussion in small groups. We do not make language groups. On the one hand, this makes things more difficult, it may be necessary to translate. But on the other, it helps since it invites people to communicate in a simple way. There is less empty talk. The linguistic diversity requires that everyone expresses in a clear and concise way what they have to say. The international discussion groups are also signs of hope: it is possible to understand each other across many borders.

The meetings outside of Taizé, in particular the European Youth Meetings as the one taking place now in Strasbourg, arose from the concern not to bind those who come to Taizé to ourselves, but to encourage them to return to their communities and churches. But then they would tell us sometimes: "It is easy for you on your nice hill of Taizé to speak as you do. We have to live, back home, under very different conditions." Out of this came the "pilgrimage of trust on earth", the European and other youth meetings. The idea was: we cannot just send the young people home and back to their churches, we must accompany them on their way back.

The last European Meetings took place, as already mentioned, in Berlin, then in Rome and now in Strasbourg. Catholic, Protestant, Free Church and Orthodox communities are hosts and find, together with us, accommodation for twenty to thirty thousand participants. Before the European Meeting in Rome a year ago, an African Meeting was held from 14 to 18 November 2012 in Rwanda. It gathered eight thousand young people, primarily from East Africa, in the Rwandan capital Kigali.

Biblical and Theological Considerations

I hope this account of experiences already allows identifying a common theme. Let me try to complete it with some biblical and theological reflections. I want to develop three points more in detail.

1. Mission and incarnation

2. Proclamation of the gospel and gathering of the church

3. Mission and kingdom of God

Mission and Incarnation

The missiology of the last decades emphasized that the Christian mission originates in God, in the *Missio Dei*. Its starting point is God sending his Son into the world. "When the fullness of time had come, God sent his Son" (Gal 4:4). The New Testament invites us to look back even further. God sent his Son at the fullness of time, when Herod was the King of the Jews and Augustus the Roman Emperor. But the decision to do so is before all time. It precedes creation. "God chose us in Christ before the foundation of the world" (Eph 1:4). Christ "was revealed at the end of the ages", but to this he was "destined before the foundation of the world" (1Pet 1:20).

If we become aware of what the *Missio Dei* includes – namely, the sending of Jesus Christ and of the Holy Spirit, the gathering of the church and even the "gathering up of all things in Christ" (Eph 1:10) – then it is plainly obvious that mission infinitely exceeds all human capacity and ability. And we are all the more amazed that Jesus Christ associates his disciples to the *Missio Dei* through the Holy Spirit. In this light it is clear that Christian mission is something different and much more than a human undertaking.

The risen Jesus said to his disciples: "As the Father has sent me, so I send you" (Jn 20:21). This means that the coming of the Son of God into the world determines what it means for us Christians to be sent. Jesus spent only a small part of his earthly life preaching the gospel with words. He spent most of it unknown by the public. He was conceived in Mary's womb, born in Bethlehem. He grew up in Nazareth and worked with his father Joseph. He spent some time with John the Baptist and his disciples. Only when he was little more than thirty years old, he went public and began to proclaim that God's kingdom is at hand.

I would like to understand the history and the life of our Taizé Community in the light of Jesus' life. Correspondences and similarities of a Christian life with the life of Jesus may show how it takes part in the *Missio Dei*.

In Taizé, everything began with prayer, work and concrete solidarity with threatened people. Prayer and work, *ora et labora*, are at the heart of monastic life since Benedict of Nursia. Monastic life refers to and emphasizes the life of Jesus before his public activity, the time when he was living in Nazareth, praying and working. Those years of his life were no less *Missio Dei*, a mission he had received from God to fulfil, than the last three years when he was preaching. The first brothers in Taizé prayed, worked and helped people who were threatened and helpless. This reminds us of what Dietrich Bonhoeffer wrote at about the same time, in May 1944: "Our being Christian today will be limited to two things: prayer and righteous action among people."

In Taizé, the gospel was always announced in the small village church and also in personal counselling. Years of common life, prayer and work let something grow and maturate which finally became public. Growth and ripening belongs to the Word of God. In Christ it did not fall from heaven, but it became man: "The Word became flesh and dwelt among us" (Jn 1:14). People could understand Jesus because he himself was born as a man and grew up, because he himself struggled to give room in his human frailty to the love of God. To be sent by him as his Father has sent him, means to be born as his little sisters and brothers, and to grow until "Christ is formed in us" (Gal 4:19). Then we become able to say his word by our lives.

Proclamation of the Gospel and Gathering of the Church

God sent his Son and his Spirit into the world in order "to gather into one the dispersed children of God" (Jn 11:52). The *Missio Dei* originates in God. God is communion, unity of the Father, the Son and the Holy Spirit. And the *Missio Dei* has its goal in the same communion and unity of the Holy Trinity. "May they all be one, as you, Father, are in me and I am in you, may they also be *in us*" (Jn 17:21). Christian life is fellowship and unity in God who is communion.

The Gospel and the Church, the good news and the gathering into community, are inseparable. Jesus proclaimed the good news and he gathered the people of God. His disciples proclaimed the kingdom of God, and, as they had previously caught fish, as fishers of men they gathered people into the community of God's kingdom. How central the gathering of the church of God was for Jesus can be learned from his saying: "Whoever does not gather with me scatters" (Mt 12:30).

In the history of the Church, unfortunately, there has been and still is a development, which does not give priority to gathering as Jesus, did. At once, it seemed to be more important to have the correct theological opinion and to convince others of it, rather than to let Christ the Shepherd "gather us into one". It is not the place to study this evolution in detail. It may be sufficient to observe how doctrinal disagreements constantly produce new churches and denominations. The problem is not the diversity, but an almost inexplicable blindness for the goal and intent of the *Missio Dei*, namely the gathering of the scattered humanity. "For Christ is our peace; in his flesh he has made both groups into one and has broken down the dividing wall, that is, the hostility between us" (Eph 2:14). And how often do we Christians rebuild dividing walls rather than participate in this work of reconciliation.

The divisions among Christians damage and flaw the gospel and the reality for which Christ gave his life, the reconciliation of humanity torn apart in hostilities into one body through the cross (cf. Eph 2:16), becomes secondary, if it is not ignored at all. The separations of the Christians make the salt of the Gospel lose its taste. How should people believe that Jesus gives free access to the love and joy he shares with the Father and the Holy Spirit, if we, his disciples, do not love one another from our hearts and sincerely rejoice in one another?

A community like our Taizé Community, too, can come into the danger or temptation to produce new separations. The desire to succeed and to gain influence is all too human. If we do not want "proclaim ourselves, but Jesus Christ as Lord" (cf. 2Cor 4:5), over and over again we must radically choose to follow Jesus on his path of service, willing to be servants of the others.

There is no salvation and reconciliation with God without reconciliation among people, and first of all among Christians. Jesus says: "When you are offering your gift at the altar, if you remember that your brother or sister has something against you, leave your gift there before the altar and go; first be reconciled to your brother or sister, and then come and offer your gift" (Mt 5:23-24). Human reconciliation is not a condition to communion with God. It is more. It is a part of the communion with God.

In Taizé, we seek nothing else than what Christians have always experienced. Listening to the word of the Gospel, praying and learning anew day after day what it means to love one another as Christ has loved us, make it possible to live together in a great diversity. Is this not a participation in the *Missio Dei*, a missional life? "By this everyone will know that you are my disciples, if you have love for one another" (Jn 13:35).

Giving priority to gathering, to communion, to unity is not an easy way. It needs infinite patience; patience with others and patience with ourselves.

Mission and the Kingdom of God

Finally, a few considerations on mission and God's kingdom are in order. The gospel, the good news, is summed up by these words: "The kingdom of God has come near." With these words, both Jesus (Mk 1:15) and his disciples (Lk 10:11) began their proclamation. In this context, "kingdom" does not have a spatial meaning; it means the actual reign, the royal rule of God. God has come near to rule the world as its king.

The Psalms celebrating the royal sovereignty of God can let us sense what this implies. Let me read some verses of Psalm 96: "Say among the nations, "The LORD is king! He has firmly established the world; it shall never be moved. He will judge the peoples with equity." (…) All the trees of the forest shall sing for joy before the LORD; for he is coming, for he is coming to judge the earth. He will judge the world with righteousness and the peoples with his truth" (Ps96:10-13).

The coming of God brings justice for all peoples; his royal rule extends to the whole world. The Book of Revelation echoes this language: "Then I heard what seemed to be the voice of a great multitude, like the sound of many waters and like the sound of mighty thunder peals, crying out, 'Hallelujah! For the Lord our God the Almighty is king'" (Rev 19:6). Jesus and his disciples proclaimed no less than God's sovereignty over all creation.

After his death and resurrection, the apostles proclaimed Jesus Christ, salvation and forgiveness in his name, and the kingdom and sovereignty of God. The last verse of Acts says of Paul: "He was proclaiming the kingdom of God and teaching about the Lord Jesus Christ with all boldness and without hindrance" (Acts 28:31). The teaching about Jesus Christ does not replace the proclamation of the kingdom of God, but confirms it: "The kingdom of the world has become the kingdom of our Lord and of his Christ, and he will reign forever and ever" (Rev 11:15). God took up his rule over the whole world together with Christ, and through Christ. Since the birth of Jesus, the peace of his kingdom is closer to us. "Peace on earth", the words of the Christmas angels, the heavenly host, are not empty words.

The missional life of the Taizé Community includes a burning desire to be associated to this aspect of the *Missio Dei* as well and to be peacemakers with Jesus who brought peace. We want the parable of our common life to also be a sign of peace. The text Brother Roger wrote for the last European Meeting in his lifetime, the Lisbon meeting in 2004/2005, bears the title: "A future of peace". He had come to Taizé at a time of war, with a concern for a future of peace and the contribution reconciled Christians can make to it. The hope for peace on earth is like a large frame around Brother Roger's life in Taizé. This hope of peace is a legacy that shapes the life in Taizé.

Just as peace on earth, solidarity among people is also a central aspect of God's royal rule and sovereignty. As mentioned before, the beginnings of Taizé have been marked by prayer and solidarity. In recent years, the question of solidarity has become important to us in a fresh way. At the meeting in Berlin, Brother Alois, the current prior of Taizé, published a text entitled "Toward a new solidarity". It accompanies the meetings up to the year 2015. In August 2015, at the occasion of the 100th birthday of Brother Roger, the 75th anniversary of his arrival in Taizé and the 10th anniversary of his death, a large "gathering of young people for a new solidarity" will be held in Taizé.

The members of the early church in Jerusalem had everything in common. In Taizé, we brothers commit ourselves to the community of material and spiritual goods. Such a life cannot be a model of society. But it can raise the question of a just distribution of wealth among people. We hope that our common life reminds us, even without words, that God has made humanity as one big family. When we pray, "Thy kingdom come", missional life as a participation in the *Missio Dei* cannot lose sight of the horizon of a new solidarity including all humanity.

Michael Dreher

Being Missional in the World of Business

I was asked to share my experiences of being *missional* and would like to do so from a specific perspective, that is, from a business perspective. I have been working in the business world for ten years. My talk is a mere short impulse. Let me begin by reflecting on how we teach and what vision we give to young people, our disciples, with regard to business. Germany is a country that is shaped by the economy. As followers of Christ, we have to think: How do we meaningfully impact the economy? And how could "Thy kingdom come …" be translated into the world of our economy?

Introduction – The Example of Nehemiah

Let me draw your attention to the book of Nehemiah. As governor of the returning Jews from their Babylonian exile he was foremost responsible for the rebuilding of the city of Jerusalem, especially the wall. In all of his work he showed a deep dependence on Jahwe in everything he accomplished (Neh 1:5ff; 3:36f; 4:3; 6:16). While it was Ezra who was responsible for the rebuilding of their house of worship, the Jerusalem temple, it was during Nehemiah's government that the law of Moses was read in the public place and the inhabitants of Jerusalem held their first Sukkot (Neh 8) after their Babylonian exile. Nehemiah was also responsible for the cleansing of the temple during his second term in Jerusalem. Therefore, what we can learn from Nehemiah's life is that

- ❑ followers of the biblical God should not withdraw from the areas of public life,

- ❑ we have to move into the public spheres of our world,

- ❑ our task is not just to focus on the church, its services and programmes for believers, but to understand that the vocation of the church is to be a church for all areas of life, because God is a God of all areas of life and not just of the church.

I know many Christians in the business world. Many of them lose their faith because they do not see their faith having any value pertaining to their work. Their faith is not working in the business life. They do not know how to live their identity in Christ. For example, when the Apostle Paul writes to the Corinthians that we are Christ's ambassadors (2Cor 5:20), or when he urges the Ephesians "to live a life worthy of the calling you have received" (Eph 4:1) then he is not restricting his admonition to their private lives. Many believers who are in the business world are somewhat disconnected from their churches because the churches do not understand what they do on a daily basis. But believers in the business realm are looking for people who would understand them; they search for role models who demonstrate that God is working through them in public life.

Our Vocation as Christians

To answer the question of how we can live our vocation as Christians, we first have to look at our calling. Essentially, I believe, there are three elements or areas that make up our calling as Christians:

First: We are called to love God and our neighbours like ourselves.

The twofold law of love constitutes the first element of our vocation. It is found in many places in the Bible. First, in the Torah: "Love the Lord your God with all your heart and with all your soul and with all your strength." (Dtn 6:5). Jesus refers to this passage in various places in the Gospels: "A new command I give you: Love one another. As I have loved you, so you must love one another. By this everyone will know that you are my disciples, if you love one another." (Jn 13:34-35 par.). Also, the Apostle Paul applies the commandment of love: "Walk in the way of love, just as Christ loved us and gave himself up for us as a fragrant offering and sacrifice to God." (Eph 5:2).

Second: We are called to proclaim the good news of Jesus Christ to the people around us.

The second element of our vocation is to walk in the mission of the Holy Spirit which is based on the mission of Jesus (Reimer 2009:139-168). Jesus said to his disciples: "Peace be with you! As the Father has sent me, I am sending you." (Jn 20:21). This, too, is emphasized in the so-called Great Commission Jesus gave to his disciples. He said to them: "Go into all the world and preach the gospel to all creation." (Mk 16:15), or in the words of the Apostle Paul: "We are therefore Christ's ambassadors, as though God were making his appeal through us. We implore you on Christ's behalf: Be reconciled to God." (2Cor 5:20).

Third: We are called to live under the lordship of Christ. That means to live under the guidance of the Holy Spirit and to act responsibly towards our world.

The third and final element of our vocation is the reign of God being realized in our personal lives. The reign of God brings the freedom to take responsibility in our own life (Rom 5:17). Revelation 5:20 states: "You have made them to be a kingdom and priests to serve our God, and they will reign on the earth." To take responsibility for the world is crucial. Like a leaven permeates the dough, so are the followers of Jesus called to permeate their environment. To me that resembles the sound of creation (Gen 1:28) which states: "Be fruitful and increase in number; fill the earth and subdue it. Rule over the fish in the sea and the birds in the sky and over every living creature that moves on the ground."

All three elements of the "kingdom of God"-vocation are for all Christians. They should be a part of God's kingdom. All elements belong together and must be lived in a holistic way under the Lordship of Jesus. This refers to individual believers as well as to the church as the fellowship of believers (Faix 2013:30-45).

Historical Influences

I moved into business when I was 16 years old. I left school early because I wanted to do something practical. I was born into a family in Württemberg that has been rooted in Pietism for generations. My mother's ancestors came from Carinthia in Austria. This is an area where Protestants were persecuted for centuries. My parents have been involved in mission work in the Carinthia region for decades. This was the setting in which I grew up. I was working in the business world but I always wanted to serve God in missions. I did not understand that to take responsibility is also a part of missions because it means to serve the people in my working place. I think we have to overcome the dualism of private and public life and to understand that there are so many people who struggle in our churches and congregations in this area.

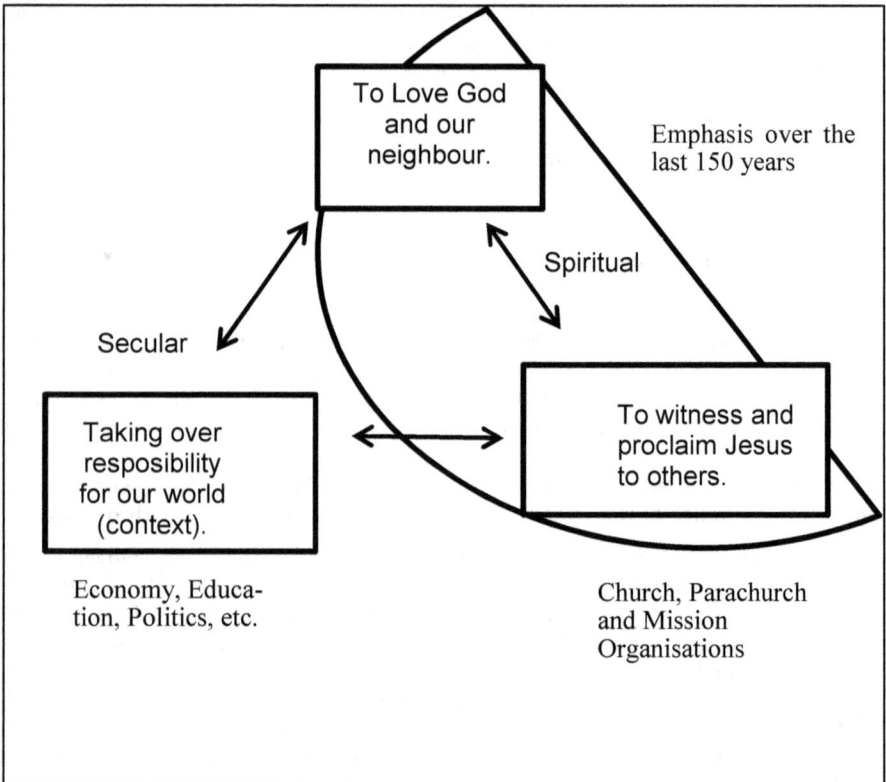

To Love God and our neighbour.

Emphasis over the last 150 years

Spiritual

Secular

Taking over resposibility for our world (context).

To witness and proclaim Jesus to others.

Economy, Education, Politics, etc.

Church, Parachurch and Mission Organisations

This dualism is the result of a historical development that happened in Württemberg and is due to the influence of Pietism. Until about 120 years ago in the older forms of the evangelical tradition (e.g. Pietism and the revival movement) all aspects of the "kingdom of God"-vocation were seen holistically together (Faix 2013:22-25). This heritage within the Christian communities has often been lost in the last 120 years. It led to a shift away from a holistic towards a one-sided focus. The focus was on the first (the twofold law of love) and the second (evangelism as implementation of the

Great Commission). The third element to govern our personal life is to perceive *and* above all to take over responsibility for the world, was largely rejected by many. The emphasis of Christians was on evangelization (inclusive church planting and church growth), personal holiness (prayer, Bible, pastoral care), and the concern for the needy (*diakonia*). These areas were defined as "spiritual". Other daily affairs of life and society were seen as "secular". The understanding of *Missio Dei* was narrowed. You can see this argument also at the exhibition here at Mission-net. You won't find many topics on business, politics, education, and so on. You will find a lot about evangelism, counselling, *diaconia* or foreign mission. This is one part of the big picture, but this is not everything. We have to bring the disconnected pieces together again. Evangelism, personal holiness and taking over responsibility for our world.

As I said, in early Pietism the element of Christian social responsibility played a much bigger role. There are many examples confirming that (e.g. Friedrich Wilhelm Raiffeisen – a social reformer and founder of the cooperative movement). Or think of the Swabian pastors Christian Adam Damm – the pioneer of animal welfare (Jung 2005), Gustav Werner – the founder of a "rescue house" for orphans and crafts operation – the "Bruderhaus Diakonie" (Göggelmann 2007), and not to forget Johann Christoph Blumhardt's ministry of healing and deliverance in Möttlingen and Bad Boll (Ising 2002). The fruit of their ministry can still be sensed in many areas of life in the place where I live 40 km south-west of Stuttgart.

Where are we today? Today, many of us think we know how to pray, evangelize, transform communities. But quite often we struggle to live the mission of God in public life and to take responsibility for the world. Is it possible to enjoy a personal, private Christianity in a "spiritual" setting, without taking responsibility for my context in which I live as a Christian? What has happened to the leaven, if he does not penetrate the dough? How do we get out of this dualism that divides life into a spiritual and secular sphere? The liberation from the resulting dualism, the distinction of a "spiritual religious communal life" from the "secular world", which you cannot get united, can only happen by the discovery of a holistic understanding of the "kingdom of God" and the associated vision.

The Kingdom of God in the Gospels

The kingdom of God is described in the Bible as leaven, light, salt or seed. Each of these elements must come into contact and interact with the physical world: the penetrated dough, the shining light, the preserving salt, and the germinating seed.

How can I show the light if I am not in the dark?

The aim of the mission of God, the *Missio Dei,* is the transformation of the world. To be part of the transformation which God creates means to be in the mission of God. To transform the world means to penetrate the world. The concept that was used in recent years for this is to live *missional.* To live *missional* in all areas and aspects of life is to proclaim the gospel of God's kingdom. This doesn't happen in a vacuum or in a purely Christian cultural environment. We have to get in contact with the context in which we live. The message of the kingdom of God can penetrate this environment, it can bring light into it, it can preserve it, and it can germinate like mustard seed.

The word "gospel" is familiar to most Christians. It means "good news". Matthew speaks in his Gospel about the "Gospel of the kingdom". "Jesus went through all the towns and villages, teaching in their synagogues, proclaiming the good news of the kingdom and healing every disease and sickness" (Mt 9:35). Word and deed are united in Jesus' ministry. It's a message that announces the kingdom of God. Where the gospel is proclaimed, the kingdom of God is established. And where it is accepted by the people they undergo a change of rule. God's *basileia* is the central theme. We can agree with Roland Hardmeier, who says: "According to the witness of the New Testament the kingdom of God is where the gospel of Jesus Christ, his deeds, his death and resurrection is proclaimed and where the kingdom breaks through with signs and wonders and where people are renewed by the Holy Spirit." (Hardmeier 2009:214 my translation).

The **motive** and the **impetus** for the proclamation of the gospel is love. God is active in mission in the world because he loves the world he created, saved it through the redemptive act of Christ's death on the cross and wants to change it. In John 3:16 Jesus is called God's gift of love to the world. The followers of Jesus are empowered by the Holy Spirit: "God's love has been poured out into our hearts through the Holy Spirit, who has been given to us." (Rom 5:5). "But you will receive power when the Holy Spirit comes on you; and you will be my witnesses in Jerusalem, and in all Judea and Samaria, and to the ends of the earth." (Acts 1:8).

The **aim** is the restoration of his rule over the world, and that his glory is made visible. God has reconciled us to him through Christ (2Cor 5:18ff). Jesus preached the proximity of the kingdom and proclaimed its presence in his own person. Repent, for the kingdom of heaven has come near." (Mt 4:17) In him God's rule is perfect. He talks, acts, does what he sees his Father doing in heaven, and establishes thereby the will of God on earth.

God establishes his kingdom – he invites people to submit to his rule. People who do that and live their identity in Christ are part of establishing the kingdom of God. It is normal for a holistic process of transformation to bring peoples into a state that God originally intended. The signs of the Kingdom are as follows:

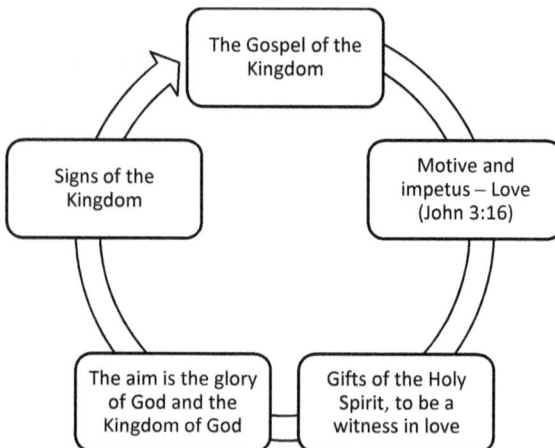

When people come out of the kingdom of darkness into the kingdom of the Son the renewal of the mind follows (Rom 12:1.2). Divine thoughts become more and more normal for his followers.

❑ The God-centered transformation of the old into the new man takes place. As a result, light comes into all areas of life and transforms everyday situations. All milieus of society are influenced or penetrated. The outcomes are transformed lives and transformed sectors of society.

❑ Exorcisms will increase, also in previously unfamiliar places, to be frank: everywhere.

❑ Healings, signs and wonders characterize the citizens of the kingdom of God anywhere at any time.

❑ The Christian's everyday life is characterized by signs, miracles and the supernatural.

Just as Jesus did what he saw his Father doing in heaven, we as his disciples will do the same deeds than he did. Jesus Christ called his disciples to bear good fruit. By these we are recognized in the world as his followers (Mt 7:16; Jn 15:16).

For further reflection:

❑ What kind of eschatology do we want to hand on to succeeding generations?

❑ How do we engage in the momentum on the sub-systems of society (e.g. economy, education, and politics)? What does the *Missio Dei* look like (Jn 20:21)?

❑ The transformation of the subsystems of society will only be achieved if we live out our identity in Christ (in word and deed). How do we hand that on to the succeeding generations? What is the role of AfeM in that?

❑ Which vision do we offer young people for their vocational choice?

Literature

Faix, Tobias. 2013. Dein Reich Komme – Gesellschaftstransformation verstehen, in: Badenberg, Robert/ Knödler, Friedemann (ed.). 2013. *Evangelisation und Transformation. „Zwei Münzen oder eine Münze mit zwei Seiten?"* Referate der Jahrestagung des Arbeitskreises für evangelikale Missiologie (AfeM). Nürnberg/Bonn: VTR/VKW, S. 19-55.

Göggelmann, Walter. 2007. *Dem Reich Gottes Raum schaffen: Königsherrschaft Christi, Eschatologie und Diakonie im Wirken von Gustav Werner* (1809-1887). Heidelberg: Winter.

Hardmeier, Roland. 2009. *Kirche ist Mission. Auf dem Weg zu einem ganzheitlichen Missionsverständnis.* Schwarzenfeld: Neufeld-Verlag.

Ising, Dieter. 2002. *Johann Christoph Blumhardt. Leben und Werk.* Göttingen: Vandenhoeck & Ruprecht.

Jung, Martin. 2005. Friede – auch unter und mit den Kreaturen: Der alttestamentliche Tierfriede in Eschatologie und Ethik des Pietismus, in: Ammermann,

Norbert / Ego, Beate / Merkel, Helmut (Hg.). 2005. *Frieden als Gabe und Aufgabe: Beiträge zur theologischen Friedensforschung.* Göttingen: Vandenhoeck & Ruprecht unipress, S. 117-127.

Reimer, Johannes. 2009. *Die Welt umarmen. Theologie des gesellschaftsrelevanten Gemeindebaus.* Transformationsstudien Band 1. Marburg: Verlag der Francke Buchhandlung.

Dieter Trefz[1]

Overview of Church Planting in Europe

Introduction

As director of a European church planting mission organization, my heart is in Europe, and for over 20 years, I have prayed for new churches and fresh church planting movements for this continent. Since this remains the focus of my sincerest prayer and desire, I would like to present to you the findings of new research on the church planting situation in Europe.

Christianity and Churches in Europe

For some time, I have been presenting Europe as a "dark continent" in terms of churches and church planting enterprises. Simply put, my message has been that Europe needs many more churches, and that it can be said to be the darkest continent in the world in terms of genuine faith. This much remains certain: mission work in Europe is exceedingly difficult, and any successes in missionary work and church planting are not easy to achieve.

This image shows the countries of Europe.

Europe – The Dark Continent

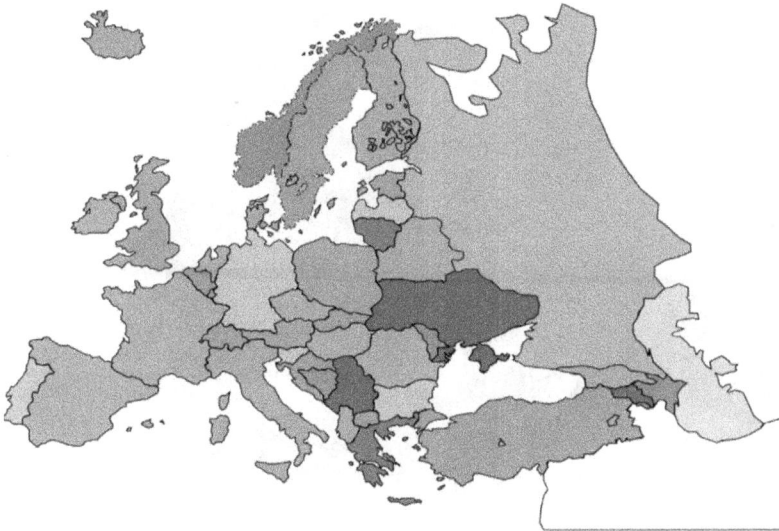

---

[1] Dieter Trefz, M.A. Missiology. Mission Director Kontaktmission, Boardmember AfeM, Vice Chairman AEM.

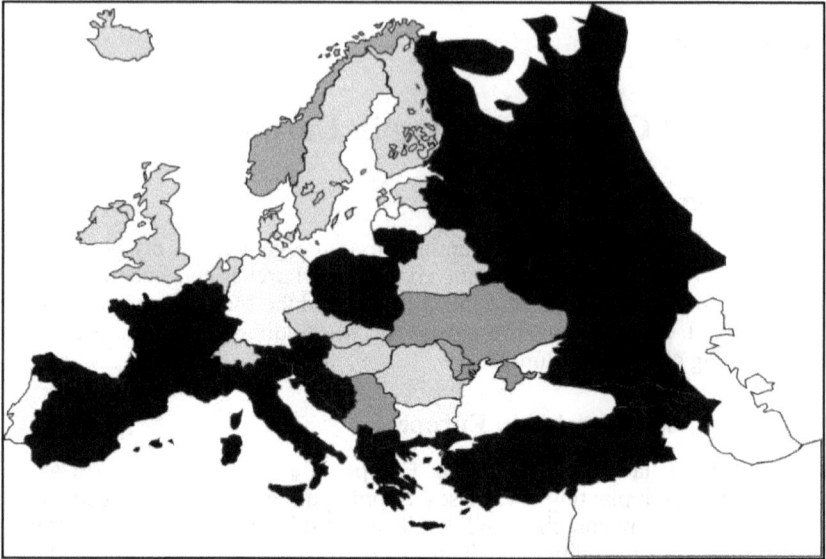

Countries with < 1% Evangelicals

The image above shows the black coloured countries in which evangelicals represent less than one percent of the population, and the image below shows the countries in which evangelicals are less than four percent of the population.

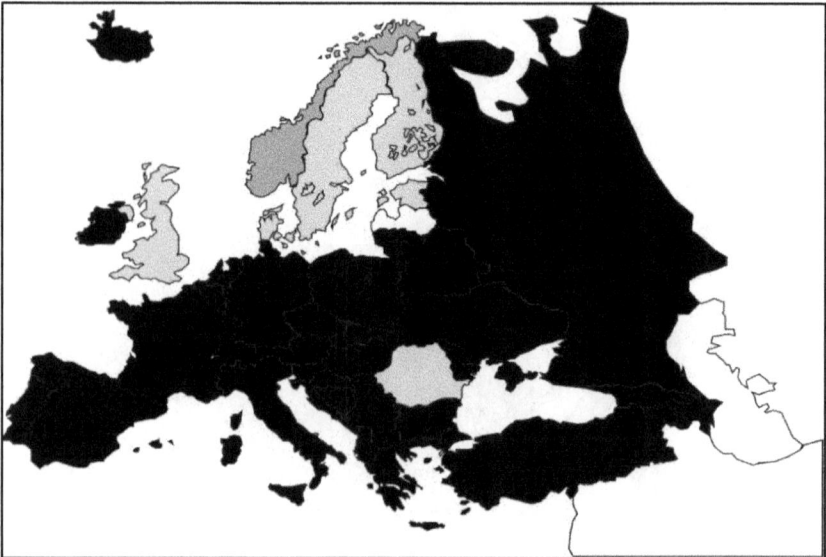

Countries with < 4% Evangelicals

But new information has come to light that challenges this view. The European Evangelical Alliance has recently stated that they can now account for 15 million European Evangelicals from 35 countries. This would indicate an average of 4.9% Evangelicals for those countries, when taken as a whole. This was the first truly positive news I had seen on this topic, and I realized I needed to correct my presentation, which showed Europe with around 3% evangelicals only.

What has been happening in Europe?

Encouraged by this new insight, I began to investigate myself, asking various missionaries and church leaders about the situation as they see it, and about what has been done in the past 20 years. I decided to focus on the countries of Russia, Lithuania, France, Austria, Spain and Portugal, because I feel these countries provide a good general impression of what is going on across Europe.

If you look for literature about Europe's church planting situation, you will discover there is quite a lot of useful material especially on strategies for planting churches. Some of these strategies come from missionaries who have left their countries of service and, as a final project, sometimes write out a strategy for reaching the country or propose ways and means how best to plant churches in that country. Here's something else to think about before looking at the results of my investigation. In his book "Church Planting Movements", David Garrison reports on three examples of church planting movements in Europe. One of them is among the Sinti and Roma; the second is a multi-cell church with its base in Switzerland; and the third is the youth church ICF, which formed in Switzerland and is now also established in Germany.

Garrison defines a church planting movement, saying:

> A simple, concise definition of a Church Planting Movement (CPM) is a rapid and multiplicative increase of indigenous churches planting churches within a given people group or population segment.[2]

Many people talk about this kind of church planting movement or CPM, and some missionaries have attempted to facilitate the formation of CPMs in Europe. They arrived with a clear vision about how the new movement should work, and about what the emphasis of their work would be. But is God actually working in this way in Europe or are current church planting movements taking shape in some other way?

Let us first examine what God is doing in Europe at present and what He has done over the last 20 years.

Some Questions about Europe

As I spoke and corresponded with missionaries and key leaders about the situation in Europe, I asked them the following questions:

---

[2] David Garrison: Church Planting Movements: How God Is Redeeming A Lost World, WIGTake Resources LLC, Monument, CO, USA (January 1, 2004).

❑ Is there a growing church planting initiative in your country? And if so, what are the emphases of this movement?

❑ Have there been "successful" church plants in the past (last ~ 20 years)?

❑ What does church planting look like today in your country?

Below I will sum up the responses to these questions in several statements and present an overview of what is going on in Europe. I will also attempt to supplement this information by providing some brief statistical snapshots. It is obviously impossible to provide a truly comprehensive overview of Europe given the limitation of this presentation. I will therefore focus on the data gathered from the countries mentioned earlier on. These examples should, I believe, greatly encourage us about the situation in Europe. Finally, I will share some observations and conclusions about this continent.

Is there a growing church planting initiative in your country? And if so, what are the emphases of this movement?

Some countries and regions have seen many churches planted, while in some countries there were only a few new churches planted, for example in Italy. In Russia, in the Volga region, there is an agreement between the local churches and churches in Ukraine to plant new Volga churches. An important goal within the agreement is for Ukrainian Christians to become increasingly motivated to go to Russia as missionaries. The Russian believers need help in missionary recruitment.

In Austria, in the years between 1960 and 1990, there was a great wave of church planting activity. At this time, the goal in Austria was to build up churches in each of the cities in Austria and also to establish a network of congregations in rural areas. One interesting development in the beginning of the strong wave of church planting was that many gifted people, for instance professional men with excellent careers, were called to serve as full-time church planters.

Have there been "successful" church plants in the past (last ~ 20 years)?

The responses to this question were very mixed. In some cases, the young churches that did come into existence were not true church plants. Rather, they arose from the division of existing congregations. The church members had come to different understandings of church, and the result was that a group of believers left the original church to start another. So, yes, Europe did wind up with some new churches, but the planting process was far from being a healthy process.

Some 10 to 15 years ago, many dynamic churches were planted in Russia. These congregations have now a membership of two to four hundred people each. However, in the last 10 years there has been a decrease in the establishment of new churches. These newer churches are smaller with congregations of perhaps fifty to one hundred people.

In other countries, we can identify a wave of church planting in the responses by missionaries and leaders. This wave can be clearly seen in the past, especially in the 90s. But in France, for example, we also find that many new churches are being planted right now.

Many new churches were planted in the eastern part of Germany after the Fall of the Wall but 10 years later, the people had already become disappointed and suspicious of Christianity. Only a few churches grew out of successful church planting projects in former East Germany.

What does church planting look like today in your country?

The following observations emerged from the responses of the survey question:

- ❑ Church planting activity is growing more quickly in cities than in rural areas.
- ❑ The planting of a new church requires at least 10 to 15 years.
- ❑ The evangelism style used today tends to be based on the forming of good relationships. The "personal relationship with people" was the clearest and most prominent answer to the question asked. In fact, it was the most common response in the entire survey.
- ❑ It takes a long time to integrate people into a new church.
- ❑ The methods and strategies for church planting vary and must be adapted to each church planting situation.
- ❑ Finding the key person who has good connections to other people is very important.

Some large churches have established daughter churches. For example, in Austria it was a long-term strategy to plant daughter churches. When a church reached around 80 members, the plan was to plant a new church. Today, the Austrian churches tend to reach a membership of about 120 people before a new church plant is envisioned.

Are there church growth statistics or church planting statistics available for your country?

In the last few years there have been many new church planting strategies applied. For most of the countries of Europe, you can find some kind of analysis about the present situation and you can find some strategies for the future. However, it is important to note that in some cases people outside the country know more about the strategies in a given country than the church planters and leaders in that country themselves.

It is interesting that in the last few years the statistics show growth and a variety of existing strategies for reaching Europe. However, the missionaries' responses to my questions show that the vast majority of "church planting movements" remain very slow projects involving many small steps.

A Look at the Progress in Church Planting in Europe

Austria

In the 1970s, the first missionaries came to Austria, but they stayed just a short time and left again. It was around this time that Austria became known as "the graveyard of missions". However, in conjunction with the efforts of local believers in and around Vienna, several churches were planted. This led directly to the establishment of the "Federation of Evangelical Churches" (BEG), which was later recognized as an official confessional community in Austria. At its inception it already had 17 member churches.

As of 2013 the BEG consisted of 45 member churches with around 5.000 members, indicating there were 28 more churches planted or added in this time. The free churches of Austria were recognized as a religious community in 2013 and a total of 160 congregations of all groups received this recognition.

Another example from Austria is the Baptists, who for many years had only 700 members in 10 churches. Since the opening of Eastern Europe, however, the number of new churches is growing, and today there are 25 Baptist churches in Austria with 1.500 members, indicating 15 new churches.

This means the BEG and the Baptists now have 43 more churches within the span of 15 years.

The Pentecostals in Austria are also seeing strong growth, primarily because of an influx of refugees since the fall of the barriers to immigration from Eastern Europe.

There are also many Romanian Christians (one of the largest churches in Austria is a Romanian church). In addition to the Romanian-focused efforts, charismatic, generally international and African-focused approaches followed.

France

In France we can notice a positive growth of protestant churches over the last 40 years. In 1970 there were only 769 evangelical churches throughout France, which grew to 2,112 churches by 2012.[3]

- ❏ 32 - 35 new churches per year or 1 new church every 10 days
- ❏ 2012: 600,000 Protestant Believers, divided in
  - ❍ 460,000 Evangelicals
  - ❍ 140,000 Lutheran-Reformed

Germany

Churches are also showing growth in Germany. The following graphic shows the traditional churches. Among them, only the Free Evangelical Church is growing.[4]

---

[3] http://www.1pour10000.fr/public_files/fck/etude_statistique_eglises_2010_daniel_liechti_cnef.pdf (19.10.2014).

[4] Own graphic, based on data from: a) www.baptisten.de (03.11.2014); b) www.emk.de (03.11.2014); and c) Christsein Heute 09/2014, Hartmut Weyel: Evangelisch und frei. Geschichte des Bundes Freier evangelischer Gemeinden in Deutschland.

Church Members

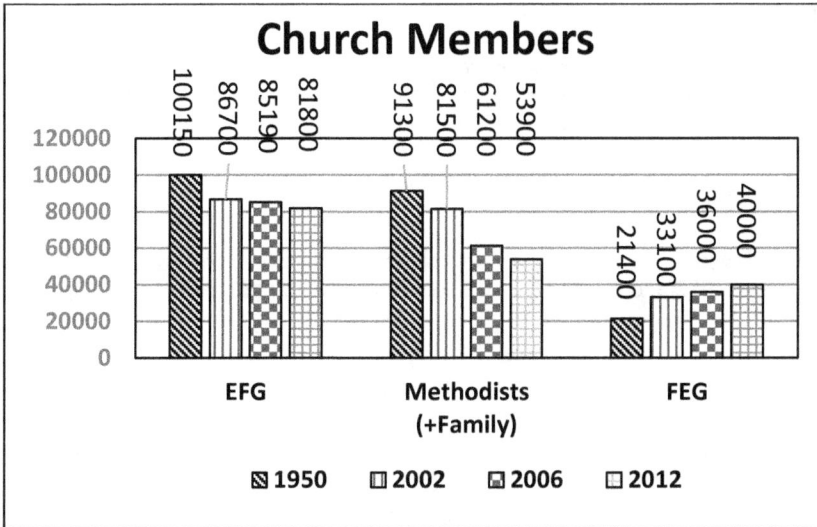

The next graphic shows the independent churches in Germany.[5] In 1994 there were around 1,000, but by 2012 there were 2,000 churches with around 150,000 members. The non-charismatic movement grew from 250 to 400 churches.

Independent Churches

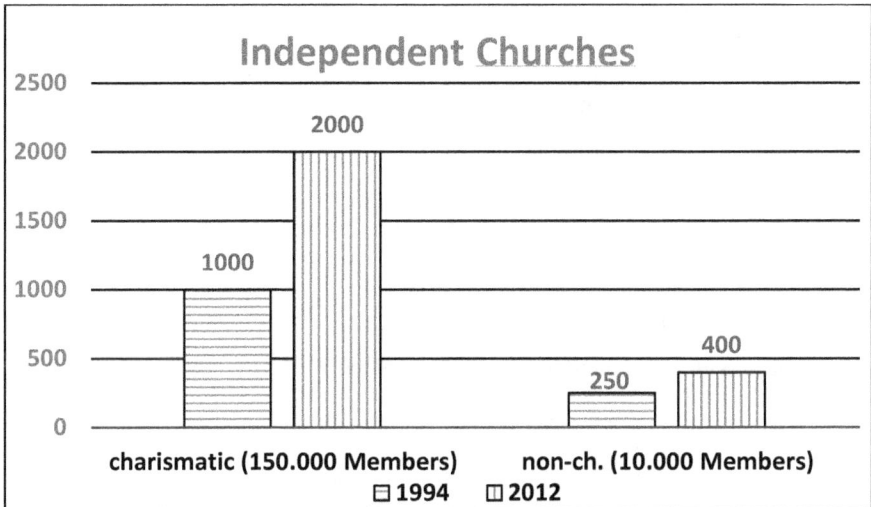

The so-called charismatic movement is growing very rapidly. Most of the immigrant churches in Germany are associated with the charismatic movement. However, in Germany some of these churches are losing members. At this time it is not clear if the new churches can grow faster than the dying churches lose members.

---

5 Idea Spektrum 24/2013

Great Britain

Since the year 2000, the British have added 5,000 new churches. Great Britain has historically been a source for many new strategies and ideas about church planting. 2,000 of the new churches were among migrants; 1,000 were Anglican and Methodist churches.

Spain

In the following chart, we can see the differences between the numbers of Spanish believers in 1982 and in 2012.[6] There are around 80,000 new believers in Spain.

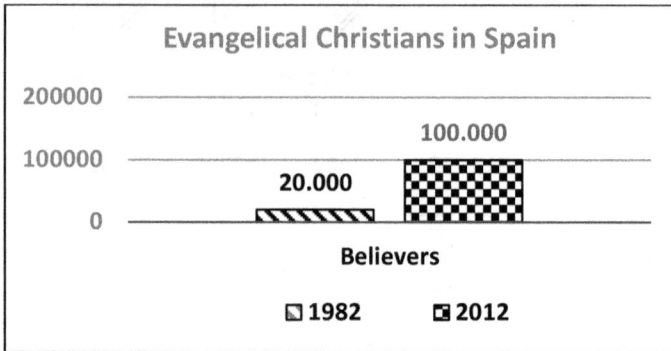

We see an especially interesting situation among the Gypsies: around 5-600,000 members of this people group live in Spain. As many as 10% of them are reported to be Christians, and up to 50% of them have access to the gospel through their families.

The beginning of the movement among Gypsies can be traced back to two of their men, who had found employment in France. They became Christians there and then went back to Spain to their people and preached the Gospel.

Immigrant Movement

Europe and Asia combined host nearly two-thirds of all international migrants worldwide. Europe remains the most popular destination with 72 million international migrants in 2013, compared to 71 million in Asia. In the past, there were many new churches in some European countries working primarily with immigrants. For example, in Spain and Italy there are many Romanian churches. One of these Romanian churches is even larger than the home church in Romania, which supported a church planting project back in Romania. Similarly, in Ireland, a team of our organization noted that some Lithuanians were not open to the Gospel in their home country, but in Ireland, they became receptive and made decisions for Christ.

---

[6] Graphics created by data of Allianz-Mission Ewersbach, Germany. http://allianz-mission.de/dienste/laender/spanien/. (31.10.2014)

At this time, I also need to mention the mission movement from the Global South. In the last ten years, we have received many missionaries from Africa and South America in Europe. This movement started in Spain and in Portugal because of the language those countries share with South America. Most of these missionaries came to find work or were invited by their people in those countries. Unfortunately, many of these missionaries had to leave because of the economic situation in southern Europe. But now this movement is more organized. A number of mission boards are working together with the mission boards in the southern continents, and they are calling missionaries to come to Europe to help in church planting. Europe has been discovered as a mission field. Many of these missionaries make statements such as, "This is our way of expressing our gratitude to Europe, because they brought us the Gospel."

Conclusions – With an Eye on the Future

The recent past has seen many new churches in Europe.

The 90s were a good decade for new churches. Austria and France saw many new churches planted, as did Germany. Overall, the past twenty years have seen many new churches spring up in Europe, but this is especially true in certain areas and countries. I observed a distinct wave of activity in the 90's and I would identify France as the country with the most new evangelical churches.

In most European countries, missionaries were the initiators of new church plants.

In general, if missionaries came to a country with a clear vision for church planting, it was fruitful for the country and many churches were planted. This is true for nearly all the Catholic European countries. At this time, more and more missionaries are working in Europe, giving us real hope for additional churches. This chart, for example, shows the German missionaries who were sent out to European locations, and we have many more missionaries from other countries and continents.[7]

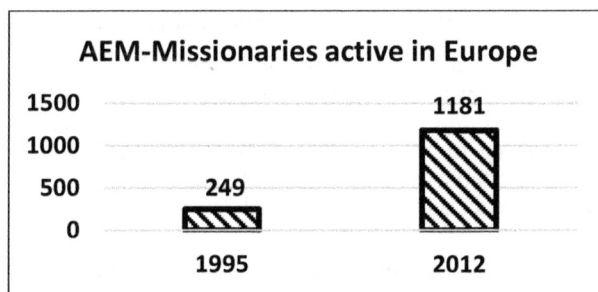

AEM-Missionaries active in Europe

	1995	2012
	249	1181

The prospect for more church plants will grow in keeping with the growth in missionary sending.

---

[7] AEM Annual Report, 2012.

In many European countries, church planters see only small advances and cannot make great leaps.

Especially in Europe, a church planter needs tremendous patience to plant a new church. Often times he/she experiences only small successes and therefore needs consistent and constant encouragement from the outside. While it is true that a typical church planter's experience is to see only small steps of growth, in most cases it is also true that in hindsight significant progress can be seen.

A new method in action.

In the 90s, the sharing of the gospel was the overwhelming priority. Today the more common method is to get involved in social projects. In one project in Portugal, for example, local believers are working to purchase land for the creation of a social centre to help people in times of severe need. And they will be able to get this land because they are well known and effective in providing social help. One church planter says he has learned not to *say* the gospel but to *share* the gospel (in practical ways). I could provide many examples of this principle in action.

The acceptance of a new church by the surrounding society is very important for reaching new people. We need more missionaries to find new ways to share the Gospel. This will help members of the host society to think about what Jesus would do in a variety of situations.

To reach the people of Europe we must use postmodern methods.

In many cases, missionaries in Europe are still trying to plant churches in some traditional way, which is an indication of their failure to understand that the context in Europe is postmodern in the extreme. This kind of culture requires a radical new thinking about appropriate methods. The almost entirely postmodern European population has often a very shallow understanding of Christianity. They have questions, but they will not naturally turn to a missionary or to the churches to get the right answers.

Working together: different approaches in different countries.

Twenty years ago, many church planters and organizations chose to work alone. Their thinking was that it was important to establish the right kind of church, or the best church. Now we find more and more frequently, that church planters are working together and learning from each other. Several years ago, a "Round Table for Church Planting" was established in Germany. In addition, since 2010 there is a national council of Evangelicals in France. Around 75% of Evangelicals are involved.

In some situations, church planting leads to a mission movement.

At the beginning of a church planting movement in a country or region, the concentration of the missionaries and churches is – and rightly so – on connecting with their own environment. But the next step, after some churches have been established, is for those churches to begin to think about mission, meaning both local church multiplication and even the sending of their own missionaries. This is happening in South America and I can see it growing in Ukraine, too. The churches in these areas desire to send missionaries to other cultures and nations.

In some countries, church planting is growing among ethnic groups.

This is happening in Germany, for example, with special ethnic groups like various South American peoples, Arabic peoples, Iranians, Turks and others. We find this same situation in several other countries too, for example in Portugal among Russians and African peoples, or in France among its various ethnic groups.

It is necessary to research and develop a new concept for each and every new church plant.

One missionary in Portugal, who has been involved in church planting for 25 years, expressed this principle in the survey. He planted four churches in Portugal and developed many concepts and strategies for new churches. In his experience, if someone wishes to start to plant a church, that church planter's first step must be to abandon the concept he used in his last church or church plant.

Engaging key individuals in the environment is central to gaining more contacts.

This is one of the most important methods identified for winning people for a new church project. Currently, most missionaries get involved in social projects and have their own natural contacts with a variety of people, but in many cases not with key individuals. But identifying and engaging just the right people is very important.

God works in waves.

In some countries across Europe, the nineties saw a true wave of church planting. In France, for example, we will see this very clearly. It is my sincere prayer that these waves of God's work will be even more powerful in the future and that they will be evident in more countries across Europe.

Final thoughts

Europe is a continent with hope. All the issues I have shared here should encourage us to move forward confidently. In fact, I even found one statistic that shows that the growth of Evangelicals in Europe is outpacing the growth of the European population at large.

My hope for Europe comes from two sources. On one hand, I trust God, and I believe that He will continue to move in Europe and that we will see results. On the other hand, I know it will help to continue to do our part by sending more missionaries to European countries. These missionaries and church planters must have a heart for Europe and they should be prepared to find exactly the right way to reach the people in each culture and location.

Connie Duarte[1]

Missional Chaos ... What are We Hoping to Produce?

A Perspective from Church Planting: A Case Study.

From Brokenness to Wholeness

The Meeting Point Experience

Meeting point was really born out of a painful leadership experience. With a 14-year old history as Estoril Baptist Church, it only took one leader to bring the church of 65-80 on a Sunday morning to 14 people within 6 months. It was a devastating experience for the church and one that almost shut the doors of the church for good.

Still, in the darkest hours of the church we could also sense the presence of God calling us to something deeper. We felt we had a choice to make. We could either disperse and each find a new place to worship; or, we could work together to be the body of Christ that we knew we ought to be. We chose the latter option. 14 members with only lay-leaders decided to keep meeting and praying together and work towards restoration and re-growth.

It did not take us long as the new leadership team to decide that we really needed a full-time leader. I, who was leading the church at the time, already had two other areas of full-time ministry that I was active in ... being a full-time pastor was impossible. Quietly I began the search for someone who could help us heal, inspire us to grow and to encourage us not to give up. 4 months later God brought the perfect person onto my radar and a few short months later, we hired a new pastor.

Goal when the Dust Settled

When the new pastor arrived and things began to "settle down" we still had to make a key decision. How would we go about restoring the church? How would we tackle the healing process? Through a lot of prayer and many discussions, we decided not to "heal" and restore the church to what it was. We decided to do something new ... which was actually something quite old!

What we really wanted to produce was a living, growing and healthy body. A body where all the parts work together to reach unity in Christ together – Ephesians 4:11.-16. We further wanted to include in our DNA the reality that a body needs to be whole and that it not only should worship together but it also ought to serve Jesus together. Therefore, we needed to teach and to live that we have a mission ... and

[1] Connie Duarte, M.A. in Leadership and Management with a major in Communications. She is married to João. They have 2 children. Her ministry experience includes 10 years with IFES in Portugal and 3 years teaching at the Baptist Theological Seminary. Currently she is co-pastor at "Meeting Point" (Estoril Baptist Church) in Portugal.

for this mission we exist! Our mission is to make Christ known ... whatever that takes, wherever we need to go and no matter what the cost.

From Chaos to Community

Our first major change was our name. We realized that for most people living in Portugal the name: Estoril Baptist Church didn't really communicate very much. It merely told people the city where we were located and our denomination, which, in Portugal, is still not understood. We wanted a name that communicated what we represented and what we wanted to do. We chose "Meeting Point" because we understood that our task was also a journey and that the journey should not be taken alone. We want people to feel like they can meet together, wherever they are on their journey, and we will walk with them from that point onwards. We want Meeting Point to be a place where we connect together but also where everyone has the chance to meet Jesus.

After the name change, we started tackling more deep rooted issues. We needed to move people from a more "traditional" church perspective into a living organism, and for that to happen we needed to help people move from living their faith **individually** to living it in **community.**

We began with encouraging and making space for being together throughout the week and sharing our lives not just on a Sunday for a couple of hours but also during the week in more natural ways. Some of the things we encourage are:

- ❑ Planning life together.
- ❑ Babysitting for each other.
- ❑ Sharing resources – financial and physical resources.
- ❑ Taking vacations together.
- ❑ Community living (if possible).
- ❑ Talking through major decisions such as changing jobs, moving community/country, etc.

Instead of these things being decided by individuals and families, they began to be talked about in community. We realized how much our individual lives affected the lives of others and therefore in many cases it just made sense to talk through these things as a body.

In our western-European mind-set we realized that most of us were very **independent** and we challenged our community to work towards becoming more **interdependent**. Therefore, we, as a leadership team, made a few adjustments to the way things were done in the past:

- ❑ We work hard at vulnerability, honesty and sharing.
  - ○ It starts with the leadership team and then trickles down to others.
  - ○ If the leadership team is not convinced and willing to do this then there is no possible way that the rest of the community is going to do it.

- ❑ We have an "all hands on deck" mentality. Yes, maybe I can do it … but should I be the one to do it … or could I ask for help? Our independent and proud nature often causes us to avoid asking for help and that leads us to over-working or working in areas that we are not gifted in. We decided that "Meeting Point" needed to allow space for everyone to be involved and to use their gifts. So many times that means we need to step back and ask for help.

- ❑ GPS groups:

  - ○ Family groups/cell groups have become a very important aspect of our community. It is in these smaller groups that the real heart-level sharing is done.

  - ○ GPS groups also allow for a "safer" place to invite friends and neighbours. Having a Bible study in a home is much less threatening for many in our communities than asking them to come to a church.

There were still other areas that "Meeting Point" needed to tackle. Much of our inheritance and tradition had lead us towards a Sacred/Secular Divide.

- ❑ We understood that we needed to move toward an integrated mission … we now teach much more clearly that every moment is sacred, all jobs are important and are from God, everything is important in God's kingdom.

- ❑ We now encourage everyone to make sure that they are taking "church" into the workplace.

  - ○ DNA groups – 2-people who meet for praying and sharing together, having lunches together.

  - ○ Being intentional in our conversations with our colleagues.

  - ○ Prayerfully working through ethical issues and counting the cost of being honest at all times.

  - ○ Changing our work schedules to make sure there is time after work to go out for coffee with colleagues and not just run home after the workday is over.

A very difficult conversation and change came when it came to our view of "what is the Gospel?" Most people had a one-word answer: "proclamation". While we want to keep proclamation a main activity of our lives, we also wanted to make sure that "Meeting Point" understands that the Gospel is Good News always and in every way. Therefore, as a church we do not limit ourselves to only proclaiming the Gospel (which we do) but also seek other ways to preach, teach and live the Good News of Jesus Christ. Here are some of the areas where Meeting Point is officially engaged:

- ❑ Serve the City (an association that feeds the homeless).

- ❑ GBU (University Study ministry).

- ❑ A Rocha (Christians in Environmental Conservation).

- ❑ Parent's Association (in Elementary schools).

- ❑ Sports (whether organized or not).

Another area that Meeting Point needed to address was how the body viewed Spiritual gifts, especially the gift of the "pastor" which had become more of a title and less of a gift! We needed to move from "Pastor as leader" to "Pastor as shepherd".

- ❑ Portugal being a Catholic country (although I have seen this in Protestant Canada too) lends itself to top-down leadership. But this type of leadership is starting to not go over very well with this generation.

- ❑ While we believe that a pastor must lead he/she ought to do it as a shepherd and not as a dictator. The results for the rest of the body have been profound.

  - ◯ By getting off the pedestal we are more able to remind people of the priestly role we have **all** been given.

  - ◯ Allowing people to have a voice, to take responsibility, to be creative, to try new things, to risk and fail has opened more doors to ministry than before.

  - ◯ We have moved from one leader to many leaders and we are now team and gift driven, rather than choosing leaders by age or by number of years in the church ... or worse yet, by income!

Another change in the way we communicated in Meeting Point was to clarify what we meant when we spoke of the "church". "Church" had often been confused with a Sunday event but we wanted to remind "Meeting Point" that "church" is really daily living and it is always.

- ❑ We started to hear (sometimes from our own mouths) things like this:

  - ◯ What time does church start?

  - ◯ When does church end?

  - ◯ What are you doing after church?

- ❑ I know what they were asking ... semantics! But we started to answer like this:

  - ◯ *What time does church start?* It started just after Easter!

  - ◯ *What time does church end?* It doesn't.

  - ◯ *What are you doing after church?* Hanging out with Jesus in Heaven.

- ❑ For us at Meeting Point Church is **ALWAYS!** There isn't a time when we aren't the church. When the celebration/service is over the Church leaves the building and enters into the world.

- ❑ The church is MOST active during the week.

  - ◯ When the Church is at work ministering to clients and co-workers.

  - ◯ When the Church is at home ministering to family and friends.

  - ◯ When Church is shopping and is ministering to clerks and other customers.

  - ◯ When the Church drives and is ministering to other drivers ... and sometimes making donations to the police department!

  - ◯ When the Church is on vacation and ministering to the environment, and to their family, friends, etc.

Moving from chaos to community has not been without a stiff learning curve, lots of trials and errors, many hours of prayer … conversations … arguments … and even laughter. While there have been many "happy endings" at Meeting Point and we are now at a point of less chaos and more community, we understand that process continues on. The church cannot become complacent and comfortable. Chaos will always exist … either inside or outside the church. How we deal with chaos will determine if we are truly a community or merely a group of individuals who meet together once or twice a week to talk about a shared belief.

Vitali Petrenko[1]

Reflections on Church Planting in Latvia

Preliminary Remarks – Setting the Stage

Just over 20 years have passed since the Soviet Union ceased to exist. As we know, this was a political system and ideology, a history permeated and characterised by its limitations regarding religious freedom, ecclesiastical life in any shape or form and missionary activities. Against this background, and on the remains of the collapsing Soviet empire, there came an unprecedented activity in terms of evangelistic out-reaches and missionary activity. The early 90s of the last century were the early years of some unprecedented opportunities, which were used with varying degrees of success. For example, I was personally involved in missionary activity and Church planting that was planned and strategically executed by our church in Riga, Latvia. As the result of these outreaches, around 10 new churches were planted in Siberia and Tyumen's region, which continue to exist, though they struggle in their endeavours.

During the subsequent 20 years of religious and political freedom, a lot of things changed in Latvia as a country and as a society. The political system changed, the economic system changed and brought about the inherent social divisions creating a chasm between those who have and those who have not.[2] Politically, Latvia is geared towards Western Europe and has orientated itself towards western culture and values. It entered the European Community (EC) in 2004 and introduced the Euro on January 1st 2014. Despite a relatively successful economic transition, Latvia has been struggling with a steep population decline since independence, as young Latvians in particular seek opportunities abroad. Between 2000 and 2011 only, the population declined by about 13% and is still declining. Currently, the population stands at around 2.1 million.

Geographically, Latvia is on the eastern border of Eastern Europe and the EC, shar-ing a common border with Estonia, Russia, Belorussia and Lithuania. That partially explains the presence of a huge segment of non-Latvian population,[3] which compli-cates the ethnic structure and fabric of Latvian society producing tension between the Latvian and non-Latvian population. About a quarter of the population is Rus-sian-speaking and the rights of this section of society have been a thorny issue since independence. Government reforms introduced in 2004 to restrict the use of the Russian language in schools remain controversial. Sadly, ethnic division along the

---

[1] Vitali Petrenko, PhD, Associate Professor, Norwegian School of Leadership and Theology, Oslo. Director of Latvian Biblical Centre, Church History, Dogmatics, Homiletics. Senior Lecturer, Greenwich School of Theology, United Kingdom. Extraordinary Senior Lecturer and Research Fel-low, Northwest University, Faculty of Theology, South Africa.

[2] 36,6% of Latvian population are on the poverty line or beyond (social exclusion) according to Eurostat in 2012. http://epp.eurostat.ec.europa.eu/portal/page/portal/statistics/search_database. (23.10.2014).

[3] Latvian 59,3%, Russian 27,8%, Belarussian 3,6%, Ukrainian 2,5%, Polish 2,4%, Lithuanian 1,3%, oth-er 3,1% (2009). https://www.cia.gov/library/publications/the-world-factbook/geos/lg.html (23.10.2014)

fault-lines of Latvian *versus* non-Latvian did not by-pass the Christian world. The contemporary churches in Latvia to a large extent exist in the mode of ethnic segregation of Latvian-speaking churches *versus* Russian-speaking churches.

Additionally, history does play a major factor in Latvia. Second World War represents the issue of contention. The two communities operate within a different historical discourse. Whilst Russian-speaking people gravitate towards Russia's perspective on victory over Nazism and celebrate the liberation of Riga and Latvia, Latvians tend to view the events of the Second World War from a different perspective, viewing Soviet troops and the liberation of Riga and Latvia as an occupation of Latvia. This perspective includes, among other factors, the acceptance of the fact of participation of Latvians in the German 'Waffen SS' (armed protective squadron of the Nazi Party) divisions and perception of these people as freedom fighters against Bolshevik's ideology and Soviet occupation. Hence, there are divergent cultural and historical perceptions, which result in annual divergent celebrations (9th of May – Russian-speaking people and 16th of March – the nationalistic march of the former SS legionnaires). This produces an annual splash of mutual animosity and antagonism in the society at large. This issue alone points towards the urgent need for reconciliation in Latvia!

Religiously, Latvia is divided between various religious affiliations: Lutheran 34.2%, Catholic 24.1%, Russian Orthodox 17.8%, other Christian denominations 1.2%.[4]

Looking retrospectively, the last 20 years produced a mixed result for different churches when it comes to the issue of Church planting and evangelisation of Latvian population. Whilst Latvian churches of different denominations grew exponentially, the Russian-speaking churches, though experiencing a fresh influx of new believers in the early 90s, came to a period of stalemate and stagnation in the 2000s. Russian-speaking churches suffered from the haemorrhage of political and religious-economic emigration of believers to the West. In some cases 95% of believers of some Russian-speaking Baptist churches emigrated to various western countries, thus decimating the resources and the potential of traditional churches. The problem is exacerbated by the fact that often the most experienced, entrepreneurial Christian leaders left. Left behind was a largely un-prepared and theologically non-educated leadership, which settled along the well-established lines of established Baptist traditions. This resulted in further isolation and marginalisation of Russian-speaking Baptist churches in Latvia. Whilst primarily isolation started in the theological realm, it brought about a cultural isolation also, resulting in a mentality of "they" and "us".

Study cases of Russian-speaking churches

With exception of two churches, the majority of 24 Russian-speaking Baptist churches are not involved in any church planting activity, only looking how to survive in the current socio-economic environment. Young and enthusiastic pastors lead the churches that are involved in outreach and church planting activity. One of the outreaches is happening in the northeastern part of Latvia, the poorest region of the country, Latgale. This church, which was built by an outstanding Latvian evan-

---

4 Source: http://en.wikipedia.org/wiki/Latvia.

gelist, William Fetler, in 1933, inherited this missionary spirit and is trying to reach the population. Three "isms" are perceived to be an obstacle on the way of effective church planting – Catholicism, atheism and occultism. Whilst Catholicism was brought onto Latvian soil by the Northern crusaders in the 12-13th Century, atheism was, and still is, the outcome of the Soviet era. The power of the occult still appears to be holding its influence, especially in the rural areas of Latgale and in some cases lurking under the garb of Catholicism, resulting in a "double-faith", in which Roman Catholicism appears to be in the fore-front of people's visible and external religious expression and the occult appears to be hidden in the background of people's lives.

The Catholic Church dominates this region and the population is very suspicious towards Protestant outreaches. The non-Catholic activity is perceived to be of a sectarian character and therefore something to be avoided. Despite the fact that in Latvia traditionally very good relationships exist between different confessions, a church planting situation or an outreach kindles the old prejudices and suspicions, causing Catholic or Russian orthodox *versus* Protestant (that is Non-Lutheran) sentiments to immediately come to the surface.

The non-traditional Protestant churches or confessions, the followers of the radical Reformation such as Baptist, Pentecostal or any other charismatic churches are widely perceived to be operating outside the cultural Latvian environment. Despite the fact that traditional churches such as Roman Catholic, Russian orthodox and Lutheran churches operate on the liturgical basis and in some cases are closely intertwined with a wider surrounding culture, the non-Lutheran Protestant churches function on the basis of a free arrangement and particular vision and education of a particular pastor or leadership of the church. However, it has to be said that there are some exceptions, in particular where some of the Baptist pastors have some leanings towards Lutheranism, if not in dogma, then, at least in their arrangements of services.

In addition to the three "isms" of Catholicism, atheism and occultism, any outreach activity in the Latgale region comes across the socio-cultural and economic reality. The population of Latgale tends to stay in single dwellings of individual farmers, which comes with a highly individualistic mentality and lifestyle. This presents a huge obstacle for any missionary or church planter in a sense that people are not predisposed to any communal gathering. Therefore, the strategy in this region is geared towards an urban setting – the small towns where there is the higher concentration of population. That in turn produced some results with three new churches appearing in and around the city of Daugavpils. Through various activities such as a soup kitchen, Bible study groups and children camps, various groups of people of different ages and nationalities responded, among them Latvians, Latgalians, Polish and even Sinti and/or Roma. It showed, at least in this case, that the Gospel can cut across national divisions and cultures, bringing unity and social cohesion in places where there is none.

Another nice exception is represented by a church-planting outreach CP-21 (Church planting 21 – in 21st Century). A young Russian-speaking pastor leads this small organization from a church plant enterprise that was planted by my church in Riga some twenty years ago. The strategy and work for church planting begun back in 1998. Though being Baptist in its outlook, the church planting strategy is designed to work across denominational boundaries, but mainly is conducted among Pentecostal, Baptist and some charismatic churches.

It is a good example of how the church planting strategy can work across ethnic and denominational boundaries and in some cases produces some amazing results in reconciliation and co-operation between two different ethnic groups and pastors of different denominations. Still, it has to be said that this program had a much better response from Pentecostal pastors rather than from Baptist pastors or from any other denomination.

One of their training bases was the city of Valmiera in the north-west of Riga, close to Estonian border, where a mixed, multi-national congregation embraced the church planting strategy and reached out beyond their city and community through various social programs and outreaches. As a result, three new congregations were established made up of different nationalities, thus giving evidence of the power and ability of the gospel to bring about unity and healing in places where there are huge divisions and alienation.

However, these examples are more exception than norm in the current environment of mutual ethnic exclusion. According to the observation of this author, the understanding of reconciliation through the power of the gospel is largely missing from the agenda and preaching of many contemporary Christian leaders. This still remains too much of a painful issue and a "taboo" to a certain extent.

Latvian Ethnic Churches

Latvian ethnic churches, though being subjected to the same politico-economic and social changes as the Russian-speaking churches, nevertheless experienced a different development in the aftermath of the collapse of the Soviet empire and its ideology. I will turn to the example of the Union of Latvian Baptist churches (ULBC).

Latvian Baptist life experienced great changes with the national awakening, which started at the end of the 1980s and the beginning of 1990s. Baptists had to learn how to live in the new economic, political and religious circumstances. It was a time of looking for a renewed identity and purpose. The new situation was seen through the words of Janis Tervits, who led the Latvian Baptist work from 1977 to 1990. He stated that during the Soviet regime, he knew how to fight "against" the Communist influence, but he did not know how to fight "for" the Church in the new circumstances. This problem was widely felt among Latvian Baptists. How to communicate the life of the Baptist churches, and how to switch from the identity of fighting "against" the external threats to that of fighting "for" the development of the Church in the new circumstances?

National and Religious Awakening

In the 1990s, many Latvians, not least Baptists, saw freedom and independence as God's will and gift. Many Latvian Baptists, together with other churches, participated actively in the process of liberalisation. In many churches, the numbers of people increased.

The old "gods" of one truth – in politics and in any other areas of life – were dethroned. Freedom of speech was a new "god" for society and for the mass media.

This new situation challenged also the Latvian Baptist Churches and the entire religious landscape of Latvia, where new ways of life sprang up almost from nowhere.

New opportunities arose for the churches to spread the Gospel by means of media and television and these opportunities to some extent were taken up. It was easy in those days to get on prime time, but some years later, this situation changed. In 1993 Baptist Bishop Janis Eisans stated that "in the past our work had been focused on inward activities because the law prohibited going outside of the church. Now was the time to think how to spread the Gospel outside the church." Christian organizations like "Campus Crusade for Christ" held evangelistic campaigns in Latvia. Evangelistic enterprises, such as "Hope – 91", "Hope – 92" brought many to Christ. Many people reached by these events later became Baptist Christians.

In 1999, the main speaker was the world-renowned evangelist Luis Palau. 150 churches were involved and more than 48.000 people attended the series of services in Riga and elsewhere. In November 2010, the "Festival Hope" with Franklin Graham as main preacher was held in Riga. This event had an attendance of about 38.000 people. These events, though bringing the evangelical preaching to the forefront of Latvian society, nevertheless, haven't brought any significant changes in terms of either new church plants or a huge number of converts into the existing churches.

Almers Ludviks, who led the evangelization work of the ULBC (1995-2001), observed that in the mid-1990s evangelistic enterprises seemed to decline in the union, though many local churches held different types of evangelism events. Perhaps any decline was due to a lack of professionalism and understanding of how to do effective evangelistic work. In addition, believers relied too much on "imported" evangelists who often were not well aware of Latvian context or culture. The ULBC in 1994 made the decision not to invite missionaries from abroad any longer but to do this on their own. Therefore, 1996 was declared the year of evangelization.

However, soon Latvian Baptists were again looking for support from abroad. Besides evangelistic events in Latvia, believers became more aware of international mission opportunities. In 1993, people from several Latvian Baptist Churches began mission work in Turkmenistan. Pastor Almers Ludviks took the key role in promoting "foreign" mission in the union. New churches were established in Turkmenistan. At the beginning of the new millennium Latvian Baptists participated in mission work in Bashkortostan, Russia, though this ministry was organized by the Latvian Evangelical Alliance with financial support from overseas. Bashkortostan was chosen because of connections the Latvians have with people who left Latvia to settle there in the 19th century.

There were also several missionary efforts in other parts of Russia. Some mission trips have been made to Estonia, but also to more distant destinations, such as Papua New Guinea. Another aspect of evangelism and mission is church planting efforts. In 2006, Bishop Pēteris Sproģis announced a vision to plant 100 churches during the following ten years in Latvia. In the year 2009, ULBC started a special church planting program following the church planting experience from Lutheran Churches in Norway. Today there are several church planting teams participating in this program and practically working in church planting. In the year 2010, the new office of vice-bishop in church planting issues was created. So far, the results have been modest, but the awareness of the need for church planting has certainly expanded in the union, which, it is hoped, will give measurable results in the future. Much hope is on the younger generation that has grown up during the last ten to fifteen years.

Finally, using this opportunity, I want to bring to your attention the fact that many pastors across different denominations in Latvia feel that the world has largely forgotten Latvia. Missionary organizations tend to concentrate their efforts and finances on the so-called 10/40 window. Perhaps not even many of you sitting in this hall know the statistics pertaining to Latvia. Perhaps it represents the equivalent of the European '10/40 window' if one is to believe European statistics where Latvia occupies one of the last or first places when one considers its demography, average income per person, etc,. etc. It does not make a happy reading. All this calls for a time of reflection, prayer and action.

Vladimir Ubeivolc

Just Missional – The Church and Social Justice: Human Trafficking

Preface

The phenomenon of poverty has been in existence from the beginning of the world. It was attested by many historical written records, which have survived until today. There have been poor and needy people at all times and in all countries. At the same time, there have always been people or groups of people aware of the seriousness of the poverty issue working hard to find a solution. Some of them went on the educational path trying to persuade people to change their world outlook, others attempted to raise people's revolutionary enthusiasm and still others were seeking to change the world by their own altruistically philanthropic example giving away their wealth to the poor.

In this article, we are going to research the phenomenon of poverty from the sociological and theological perspectives in the East European context.

Over the last hundred years, the Church became more concerned about the poverty issue, although it should be noted that the practical assistance to the needy has always been a part of the Church service. Nowadays, theology and missiology are also worried about the extent of the problem. More and more often, missiological and charitable agencies as well as such influential alliances as the World Evangelical Alliance and the Baptist World Alliance put the poverty problem-solving question on their agendas.

Several generations of Christians each at their turn, hoped to see this problem solved with their own eyes. Nowadays, there are new methodologies, approaches, and concepts but unfortunately, they do not bring a change to the existing state of affairs. Moreover, the poverty problem becomes more serious and in many regions of the world, the situation is even critical. Unemployment, the economic and social instability, unrealistic expectations and the collapse of dreams are intensifying the process of people marginalization. The state of poverty does not allow society to realize its potential opportunities and consequently, it slows down its development. This is why poverty is associated with social development regression.

At the same time, researching the human trafficking issue, I notice obviously at least the bipolarity of the causes of this problem. On one hand, there is a demand for cheap slave force (sexual or work). On the other hand, there is the offer. This one usually comes from the context of poverty while the demand is universal. The example of the modern Europe is an illustrative one in this case. Despite the crises, Western and Northern Europe are still attractive to different kinds of migrants. Eastern Europe is trying hard to integrate into the "Old Europe" and very often, the integration is due to migrant flows from East to West and North as well as to the financial flow from North and West to East instead of being due to internal systemic changes within Eastern European countries.

The human trafficking issue is so closely related to the poverty issue that it is impossible to characterize these two phenomena in detail just in one chapter. Nevertheless, in my opinion, it would be difficult to give a characterisation of the poverty phenomenon and its relation with human trafficking even if there was enough space. All the same, the Church simply does not have the right to remain silent on this issue as the stratification of the society and the increasingly noticeable gap between rich and poor people create more and more new issues. They not only concern a part of the mission of the Church, but directly the local churches, the lives of believers, and even have an impact on the internal church structures.

The present study is going to tackle issues like approaches to poverty definition, causes and criteria of poverty and theology of poverty as well as is going to suggest practical recommendations to churches so that they could include the issue in the missiological vision of their church.

Definition of Poverty

It is not easy to give the definition of poverty, as the concept itself is relative. There is no unique explanation of poverty. The poor are always compared to the rich people. Thus, in its broadest sense, poverty is the condition when there is a discrepancy between an average level of means for proper existence and the possibilities of meeting these needs within some specific group of people. In other words, there is a certain average consumer level, there are those whose consumption basket is by far above average and … there are those who do not reach the average level. The latter are referred to as poor.

Moreover, the average level may differ depending on the country. For instance, if we compare the average consumption level of Norway or Sweden to that of Ukraine or Moldova it will appear to be very different. Otherwise, if comparing the same high average level to that of India or Tajikistan, the data will differ even more. The condition of the poor in a country differs from the condition of the poor from other countries and from the condition of the rich people from their own country. While the life of the rich people is similar in most of the countries, that of the poor people varies substantially. The poor build their own life values, ethical principles and frequently their own slang. In other words, these are the characteristics of a subculture. Subcultures are usually peaceful, but sometimes they may pose a threat to the existing social order and in separate cases even wipe it out (Russia 1917, Egypt and Libya 2011, etc.).

At the same time it is indisputable that the concept of "poverty" should not be defined only from the financial point of view. Jesus Himself was talking about those "poor in spirit" (Mt 5:3). Nowadays, the phrase "spiritually rich person" is very popular. The Orthodox Church as well as some Catholic orders (Franciscans, for example) consider people who have voluntarily given away all their material goods as spiritually rich people. Therefore, speaking about poverty, we should keep in mind such components as worldview, social relations, the education level, the access to basic means for proper existence (clean water, housing, clothing and food) and health care.

In the various typologies adopted as the basis of social stratification, it is told about the so-called "lower class". The well-known American sociologist Watson speaks of the "highest-lower class" and of the "lower-lower class". The first group comprises wageworkers who are financially relatively stable, but are in constant dependency on the upper classes with regard to their income as well as having limited access to quality education. The second one includes the poor, homeless, unemployed, etc. I would add to this second group the illegal migrants. Some sociologists have also expanded the second list incorporating the people whose income constitutes less than half of the income of the average full-time industrial worker.

In Eastern Europe, and especially in those territories, which until 1991 were part of the Soviet Union, the phenomenon of poverty is even more diverse. Here are some examples. A large part of adult citizens, who had been working for many years in state-owned enterprises, got apartments free. During the Soviet era people could neither sell nor buy those apartments but after the collapse of the Soviet Union they began to privatize them actively and practically all the apartments turned into private property. To date, the cost of a small apartment (two rooms with an area of 30 square meters) in cities such as Chisinau can cost up to fifty thousand Euros. The same size apartment in the centre of Moscow can cost up to half a million euros. Considerable parts of people who have benefitted from free apartments are now retired. And we can hardly call a person who owns a real estate worth 50-100 thousand Euros poor. At the same time, the monthly income of a family of pensioners in Chisinau can amount to less than 150 Euros, given that the cost of the utilities (electricity, water, etc.) can exceed 200 Euros in winter. Nevertheless, those people do not have the opportunity to sell their flats and move to cheaper ones. In fact, they have to choose between dying of hunger and not paying the bills running the risk having electricity, water and gas supply cut off.

Here is another example illustrating the life of rural people from Moldova for whom it is practically impossible to find a paid job. Twenty years ago, the big majority of these people were working for the state. It is difficult for them to set up their own business because: 1) they lack entrepreneurial spirit, which was suppressed during the Soviet era, and was not inculcated during the years of independence, 2) the unfavourable tax laws, which are lined up in favour of large companies and enterprises, and is nearly strangling the small business. People are forced to seek places of work outside their community, and frequently, outside their country. Moldavians leave their country mostly for Russia and Italy. Almost one million Moldavians work abroad (around 30% of the whole population). On average, one of the parents from almost every family is working abroad. There are also thousands of families where both husband and wife work outside the country. In many cases, they work in different countries. Thus, their children are left alone without parental care. As a rule, parents do not arrange for guardianship of someone from the family, trying to avoid additional bureaucracy. Children are left to themselves. Parents send them a monthly financial support of several hundred Euros. As a result, two teenagers, a girl of about fourteen and a boy of about twelve, live in a house and have enough money to pay for commodities, food and even entertainment. But they are completely deprived of parental control, care, love and communication. Naturally, this leads to the impoverishment of their emotional and social world. The critical questions, which arise in this situation, are as follows: Can we say that these children are well off? Are they poor?

Referring to the classification of poverty, it is worth noting that there are whole classes and groups of people who cannot meet basic physiological needs. They are followed by those who have enough material resources to meet their basic needs, but do not have access to social benefits (restriction of access to education, medical care, recreation). There are also those who consider themselves poor, even though they have no need of any material or social benefits. Their arguments are based on the comparative analysis of the quality of the benefits they receive. For example, they have food, but it is not of high quality or they have a shelter, but it does not allow them to have a so-called "private" space. In addition, it is important to point out the phenomenon of "intellectual poverty". There is a category of people who have managed to break the cycle of poverty (for example, on the basis of unequal social marriage). But while they have access to all kinds of benefits they cannot get used to them and behave as the poor (e.g. they overeat for fear of lacking food the next day, they over-save appliances and household items using the old ones and storing the new ones for "the black day", etc.). In Romanian, there is a saying: "the one who was hungry for three days, remains hungry forever."

By taking into account only the financial perspective, we can identify at least two levels of poverty: absolute poverty, from which, according to official data for 2010 in Moldova, about 22% of the population suffer (their income is less than 70 Euros per month) and extreme poverty from which about 2% of the Moldavian people suffer (their income is less than 30 Euros per month). The data for 2011 show that about one-third of the population live below the poverty line. Moldovans spend eight times less money on health care than on food and thirty-nine times less on education than on food. Thus, the major part of the income is spent just to survive. This fact mainly influences the relatively low life expectancy in Moldova. Men live on average 65 years and women 72 (both men and women live on average 68 years) whereas in Sweden and Italy the average life expectancy is about 80 years, and in Belgium and Greece it is around 78 years.

About 80% of the poor Moldavians live in rural areas. It should be noted that there are two forms of poverty: stable and mobile. The first is related to the fact that the low level of social security, as a rule, leads to poor health, disqualification, loss of professional skills, and ultimately to degradation. Poor parents give birth to potentially poor children, as determined by their health, education, qualifications. People who are born "persistently poor" remain poor throughout their lives. The second form is much rarer, because poor people are making extraordinary efforts and break out of their social class, adapting to new conditions. Naturally, not only the subjective, personal factors play a part in such kind of changes, but also the objective conditions created by the state and society. It happens that the rich become poor. In Eastern Europe, many of these cases were noted during the change of regime in the early 90s. Then, the most considerable part of the society had a privileged position based on the civil service, status and party affiliation. With the collapse of the socialist system, those people lost their source of income, their position and the opportunity for career advancement in just one day. Many of them were not able to cope with the new realities of life.

When tackling the subject of absolute poverty, it is impossible not to mention such a concept as relative poverty. The definition of poverty is relative because it is based on the comparison of the living standards of poor people from one country (or one region) with the poor from another country (or region). In the 70-80s, Liberation Theology was trying to attract people's attention to this discrepancy. It was focusing on the fact that today's rich countries obtained their status due to the centuries of colonization of the "third world", and thus, it was calling for a redistribution of wealth between countries and continents.

The last phenomenon, which should be mentioned in this context, is the poverty of vulnerable people. There are poor who have lost their wealth because of different reasons: a change of system, bankruptcy, crisis, alcoholism, etc. But under favourable circumstances, these people can rise above the poverty line and start a new life. There is also a category of the poor in Eastern Europe, who do not have chances to escape from the circle of poverty in the near future. These are people with serious injuries, lonely pensioners, and in some countries, orphans can also be part of this category. The whole state and social system is set up so that powerful people supplant the weak ones. The State can help this category of people only to meet their elementary physiological needs. The civil society is trying to do everything in its power, but lacking government subsidies, it can provide only individual, local and temporary assistance.

A particular attention should be paid to the issue of abandonment in Eastern Europe. In Russia, for example, there is a state program designed to guarantee housing to all orphans aged eighteen. We cannot say that it works flawlessly, but at least it is available. In Ukraine, there is the movement "Ukraine without orphans", which counted the number of all Christian churches and organizations in Ukraine, as well as the number of orphans. It turned out that these two figures are almost equal. The movement puts the emphasis on the adoption of at least one orphan by every Christian church. In case of Moldova, a state program has been launched aimed at eliminating the boarding schools. The purpose of the program is to encourage families to adopt orphans. But families can hardly benefit from any assistance. Many temporary Care Centres for orphans have been opened recently. Children are looked after there for only six months. During this period, it is expected that families eventually adopt them. In practice, children spend six months in a centre, then, they are transferred to another one and so on.

The NGO "Beginning of Life", where I serve as president, runs a rehabilitation centre for the survivors from human trafficking and sexual exploitation. Between 2009 and 2012, the Centre sheltered about 40 women. More than 30 of them are orphans. Most of the orphans do not have access to full secondary education. Thus, they do not have any opportunities to benefit from higher education, and therefore to have a prestigious job in the future. The maximum they can afford are vocational trade schools, where they are taught professions which are not in demand in Moldova, or are underpaid. During the training, orphans live in hostels but after graduating, even in the case they find a job, their income is not enough to rent a habitation. They are forced to live in dens, to unite in large groups (often mixed-gender ones). Thus, they become easy targets for pimps, traffickers and recruiters.

The research we have carried out allows us to give a concise definition of poverty. Thus, poverty is a characteristic of poor individuals who cannot meet their basic needs according to the average level of life satisfaction.

Causes of Poverty

The problem of poverty is related to social forms of alienation of people from each other or from society, from the prerequisites and the results of work, from the work itself. It is characterized by a significant restriction of basic goods consumption and the formation of an environment in which the subculture of the poor becomes a destabilizing factor for society.

Earlier on we have already highlighted some personal causes of poverty. The following section puts emphasis on some of the systemic causes of poverty.

The Crisis of the Political System

We have already mentioned that one of the most striking events of the period after the Second World War in Europe was the collapse of the Soviet Union. It changed the life of people living there in every way. The map of Europe was redrawn with catastrophic consequences. It is unlikely that Christians who were praying for decades for the fall of the Iron Curtain, the elimination of the totalitarian regime in the Soviet Union, could imagine the consequences that were to follow the event.

Besides the fact that wars broke out, thousands of people committed suicide, millions of others lost their jobs, and, consequently, their means of existence. Having a dualistic worldview, we think that the fall of the USSR brought positive change as Christians became free to express their faith. However, if we examine the issue from a holistic point of view, we cannot definitely state that the process was a very good one. After all, hundreds of women who sell themselves on the streets and brothels of the European Union went out of the former socialist countries (Bulgaria, Romania, Ukraine, Moldova, Russia, etc.). Or take the spread of the Russian mafia in Prague, Warsaw or New York made possible when borders opened and millions of unemployed Eastern European rushed abroad only wishing to survive. Unfortunately, such processes continue. The revolution in the Arab world can have such consequences, consequences that European countries could not even imagine. This happens hardly because politicians did not make the right conclusions. It is likely that the recurrence of such processes is clearly advantageous to certain circles. The millions of refugees and illegal migrants on the one hand, represent a threat to wealthier countries while on the other hand, they represent a source of cheap labour force and provide a market for substandard and outdated products as well as girls and women for the sex industry.

The Economic Crisis

It is difficult to study the global economic crisis at the time when it started and it is not likely to stop. The U.S. financial crisis, the stock markets, the weakening of the hard currencies, the long-lasting problems of Greece, Italy, Ireland, Portugal, Spain and other European countries, show that the situation is far from under control. People lose their jobs and within the EU, there is a growth of the so-called lower-middle class and the upper-lower class at the expense of the decrease of the higher-middle class.

Hundreds of thousands of people from the new EU member countries (Romania and Bulgaria) have rushed to the West and the North in search of better jobs. Social ties are broken and the risk of exploitation of some people by others increases. Again, the most in demand and most well paid activity – one that does not require additional skills – is the human trafficking. Men and women are sold because not only are they overwhelmed by their financial needs, but also because it is possible due to the weakening of traditional family ties. The social and financial poverty levels bring people onto the streets.

Social Isolation

Having left their usual environment, certain individuals and groups of people face a completely different culture to which they cannot get used to for years. Being actually isolated, many of them choose to communicate with their close people by means of the Internet. Nevertheless, such kind of communication does not lead to social security. More and more people become lonely. Thus, their social capital is reducing from year to year. They do not keep in touch with their old acquaintances, and do not make new ones. In case of accidents, emergencies or illnesses, these people are on their own and have nobody to turn to and to ask for help. And even if the state or the company incurs financial compensation, this is not enough to help people meet their basic needs. Only a very small number of people can really be helped.

Criminal and Social Threats

The arms and drug trafficking becomes a more and more profitable business with every year. Only in 2011 in Moldova, the official arms trade has increased by over 100% compared to 2010 and 95% of the people buying guns say that they do it primarily because they are uncertain about the future. In addition, people own a huge number of unregistered weapons bought in the 90s. All these factors increase the crime potential in the country and consequently, the number of the committed crimes is increasing every year.

Drug addiction makes masses of young people fall into the category of marginal subcultures. Most of them are unemployed and their unique source of income is drug selling and criminal activity.

A new generation of orphans from Eastern Europe, whose parents are working in the EU countries for many years, will become a real threat in only a few years from now not only for Moldova, but for the whole of Europe. Given that nearly 800,000 of Moldavian citizens appealed to the Romanian Consulate to obtain the Romanian citizenship, we can assume that in a few years, most of them will go to one of the EU countries.

There are, actually, many causes of poverty. We have tried to give a systemic explanation of the given phenomenon without taking into account the subjective and the personal factors.

Theology of Poverty

While studying the phenomenon of poverty, we do not have the right to circumvent the biblical perspective on the problem of poverty and the response of the church to the presence of this problem in modern society. I would like to draw attention to the words of Christ, to His teachings, which have its theological foundation in the Old Testament. They open a slightly different perspective and are associated with His personality and ministry.

I want to concentrate on a very important text in the theological and sociological discussion, taking place in the heart of different theological schools, based on Luke 4, which shows the role of marginalized people in Jesus' ministry.

This text is interesting due to one main reason – it is a reminder of Jesus about the poor to whom He came to preach the good news. In all the countries of Eastern Europe the society got divided into rich and poor. It is necessary to note that among the evangelical churches there are also more wealthy people now than formerly. Still the majority of the inhabitants of these countries are miserable and poor.

I would especially like to mention the situation in Moldova. It is important to pay attention to a dual phenomenon of this country. Firstly – from 1990 until 2000, the quantity of the members of evangelical churches at least doubled. Secondly – during these years, Moldova became the poorest country in Europe. Thus, the evangelical churches are facing an urgent need to formulate a response to the poverty issue in this country.

Jesus begins to cite the prophet Isaiah (61:1). The words "The Spirit of the Lord is upon Me" emphasize not just the special importance of the words that follow (similar to the words "The word of the Lord that came to the prophet." [Micah 1:1; Hosea 1:1; Joel 1:1]), but also talk about an undeniable authority.

In the last thirty years, these specific words of Jesus ('because He has anointed me to preach the gospel to the poor') became the object of the most heated discussions among theologians. What kind of poor people does Jesus refer to? And depending on the answer, the term "to preach the gospel" also gets a specific meaning. For one group of poor people the Good News consists of one thing and for the other one – of something else. Some of the greatest missiologists of the 20th century think that the Good News of the Kingdom is that the whole of Christ's work is a work of liberation from the rule of sin, Satan, and death. Hence, the church must reflect liberation from the influence of the 'dominion of darkness'.

It is hard to answer the question: who is "poor"? With: this is the lowest economic class of the society. "In the Old Testament the poor are not the ones who are economically poor people, but the ones who have lived in a complete dependence upon God". D. Dorr, in his turn, also with references to the Old Testament, comes to the following conclusion: "The term refers to those groups of people who are economically deprived, who have no social status, and who are treated unjustly by foreign rulers or by the authorities in their own land."[1]

Th. Houston, one of the leaders of the Lausanne movement, pays attention not to the Old Testament understanding of the concept "poor or needy" but addresses the study of the Old Greek language: "The two words used for 'the poor' in the New Testament are *penes* and *ptochos*. *Penes* refers to the person who is oppressed, underpaid, and the working poor. *Ptochos* refers to the person who has no work to do and has to beg."[2] D. Bosch said: '*Ptochos* – is a generalizing concept to cover all the unhappy people'.[3]

---

[1]   Donald Dorr. 2000. *Mission in Today's World.* (Maryknoll, NY: Orbis Books), 151.

[2]   Tom Houston. 1989. 'Good News for the Poor', in *Proclaim Christ until He Comes: Calling the Whole Church to Take the Whole Gospel to the Whole World, International Congress on World Evangelization 1989* (Lausanne Committee, 1989), 155.

[3]   David J. Bosch. 1998. *Transforming Mission: Paradigm Shifts in Theology of Mission.* (Maryknoll,

Luke, as no other evangelist, spends a lot of time on the issue of the poor and the rich (1:53; 3:12-14; 7:11-17; 18:2-5; Acts 11:27-30). Agreeing with Bosch, a question remains: "What kind of good news did these poor people need?" We can answer this question with Th. Houston's words: "It was the kind of Good News that brought a prostitute to wash Jesus' feet with her tears and wipe them with her hair, and then Jesus say, 'Your sins are forgiven' (Luke 7:36-50, TEV)". Furthermore, "The Good News of the kingdom of God is that sin, disease, and oppression are never the last word. Where Jesus is King, he brings forgiveness, healing, and liberation."[4]

The Spirit of the Lord has anointed Him to preach the gospel to the poor. Anointing in the Old Testament was used in order to separate one for a special mission, all the other components of Jesus' mission are accompanied by the verb "sent". He sent me to heal the broken-hearted. It is interesting to mention that the commentators refer the least about the broken-hearted. That is more likely because this phrase cannot be understood in a poly-semantic way. The broken-hearted are the ones who, due to different reasons, got an emotional, psychological (or as people call it "heart") wound. This can be due to poverty as well as other various reasons (loss of close ones, war, famine, natural disasters, unshared love, poverty, etc.). All these categories of people need a healing of their hearts, settling of peace in their hearts.

Some commentators see a parallel between the phrases "to preach deliverance to the captives" and "to set at liberty them that are bruised". And the discussion again develops around the issue if these words had a physical or spiritual meaning.

Then Jesus announces that He came to preach the acceptable year of the Lord. This is the year that according to Moses' law was celebrated only once in every 50 years, a year, in which all debts were forgiven, slaves were set free, and land taken under guarantee, was being returned back to the owners (Lev 25).

Jesus said that "today this scripture is being fulfilled in your eyes" after the people were already looking at Him with surprise. The fulfilment of the Scriptures talked about the fact that liberation will come, but the confusion arose because they were waiting to see it in a different form. This one-way declaration of Jesus does not leave any doubts that He was the long awaited Messiah of Israel.

Conclusion

The threat of poverty looms over certain socio-professional groups of citizens. "The social bottom" absorbs farmers, unskilled workers, engineers, teachers, intellectuals and scientists. Within society, an effective mechanism makes people effectively reach the "bottom". It mainly consists of the current methods of carrying out the economic reforms, the unrestrained activities of criminal organizations and the state's inability to protect its citizens.

The ideal purpose of the strategy aiming at the reduction of the absolute poverty is to overcome it totally. In a healthy society, and especially in a social state, people should not live below the subsistence level. The purpose of the fight against the rela-

NY: Orbis Books), 99, 435.
[4] Tom Houston, 'Good News for the Poor', 156.

tive poverty is not the complete elimination of inequality, but its optimization, its reduction to a level which does not exceed the acceptable limits in a given society and at the same time, which does not undermine the incentives of social and economic activity. The main weapon against poverty is such a policy, which would be aimed at the economic growth of the country.

The task of the Church, in this case, does not consist only in helping the poor who found themselves at the very bottom of society, but also to get involved in the prevention of poverty at the society, state, and even multinational levels.

Thomas Schirrmacher[1]

A New Horizon of World Christianity

Convergence between the Ecumenical and Evangelical Understandings of Unity and Mission!?

Since the 2013 annual meeting of the World Council of Churches and the 2014 General Assembly of the World Evangelical Alliance were planned to take place in South Korea, Korea's Christian Academy of Sciences invited these two global church affiliations to an official dialogue on the topic "A New Horizon for World Christianity: The Convergence between the Ecumenical and Evangelical Understandings of Unity and Mission", with 300 theology professors in attendance.

In his address, which is being presented here in an updated version, the main representative of the World Evangelical Alliance (WEA), Thomas Schirrmacher, traced the history of the relationship between the two bodies and pointed out where the main differences lie. A portion of these differences have been largely set aside by the end of the Cold War and the shift of world Christianity to the Global South. This facilitates cooperation and generates hope that the remaining differences will not only be taken seriously, but also worked off in a self-critical manner.

Thus, a leading representative of one of the three global Christian bodies describes how the relationship between his body, the WEA, to the other body of the same size, the World Council of Churches (WCC), has changed since the beginning of the new millennium. He describes the major areas of disagreement in the second half of the 20th century, and discusses in which areas both sides come closer to each other, and which areas of disagreement need yet to be worked on.

Christian Witness in a Multi-Religious World (2011)

"Today represents a historic moment in our shared Christian witness," claimed Jean-Louis Cardinal Tauran, president of the Pontifical Council for Interreligious Dialogue on 29th of June 2011 at the launch of the ecumenical ethics code for mission

---

[1] Thomas Schirrmacher, PhD, ThD, DD, earned his doctorates in missiology, cultural anthropology, ethics, and in the sociology of religion. He is chair of the Theological Commission of the World Evangelical Alliance (WEA), director of the International Institute for Religious Freedom (Bonn, Cape Town, Colombo) of WEA and speaker for human rights of WEA, speaking for approx. 600 million Christians.

He is professor of Sociology of Religion at the State University of the West in Timisoara (Romania) and Distinguished Professor of Global Ethics and International Development at William Carey University in Shillong (Meghalaya, India), as well as president of Martin Bucer European Theological Seminary and Research Institutes with branches in Bonn, Berlin, Zurich, Innsbruck, Prague, Istanbul and Sao Paolo. He is chair of the Association of Evangelical Missiology (afem) and a member of the board of the International Society for Human Rights. He regularly testifies in the German parliament, the EU parliament and the OSCE. He authored and edited 102 books. His newest books include 'Fundamentalism', 'Racism', 'Human Trafficking', 'Human Rights' and 'Missio Dei'.

"Christian Witness in a Multireligious World". For the first time in history the Vatican, the WCC, and the WEA issued a joint document, representing approximately 95% of Christianity.

The very first words in the preamble state: "Mission belongs to the very being of the church. Proclaiming the word of God and witnessing to the world is essential for every Christian. At the same time, it is necessary to do so according to gospel principles, with full respect and love for all human beings."

Therefore, we could stop our topic here, as this preamble seems to bring decades of discussion between the WCC and the WEA to an end towards convergence in mission. Or were these only nice words and a typical diplomatic statement with no real meaning?

A press release from that day reported my evaluation at the launch:

> Thomas Schirrmacher, who coordinated the efforts for the World Evangelical Alliance, made it clear that the document presented is in no way a compromise. Over the years, there have been very sceptical voices from assorted directions which held a document with any substantial content regarding the topics of freedom of religion and mission as impossible to compose. In the end, there are now distinct recommendations, which on the one hand, clearly bear witness to Jesus' mandate to his church. On the other hand, there are also limits highlighted with respect to mission tied to the biblical message, and religious freedom and human rights are seen as the other side of the coin of mission.

The time in which it was discussed whether the age of world mission was only a matter of history seems to be history itself. Even though the "moratorium on missions", called for at WCC's world mission conference in Bangkok 1973, meant for many only to reduce the number of *Western* missionaries, it seems to come from another age when compared to the new document.

Let us for a moment leave aside the fact that the Vatican in this case acted together with both bodies. Actually, the Vatican saw only two actors here, the Catholic Church and the rest of Christianity – that is to say, the WCC and the WEA represented all other churches, with an equal number of combined members as the 1.2 billion members of the Roman Catholic Church.

Which changes in the last decades have made it possible for the WCC and the WEA to converge in certain aspects of world mission and in other areas of church and society? Let us first go back to the founding phases of the WCC and the WEA and then discuss the last two decades. Of course, I cannot go into any detail here and only want to offer some propositions for understanding and discussion.

I also want to warn you: due to space restrictions and the fact that this is not a scholarly piece, I will generalize frequently and only discuss major tendencies and trends. Perhaps this is also due to my German nature, as we German's always try to find the deepest principles behind everything, not the stories that actually make history come alive ...

History of the WEA and the WCC

Neither the WCC nor the WEA have an even, linear history, but histories with difficulties and several very different streams from history coming together. They both grew gradually by including older ecumenical initiatives and global organizations, which again have their own history. They both mirror the world around them in the last six decades since World War II. The WEA had to suffer from a split between Europeans and US-Americans at several points. The respective regional and national histories of the branches of WCC and WEA are very diverse, not to speak of the diverse histories of all its member churches.

However, in the development of both bodies I find four common central topics going back into the early history:

❑ *The unity of Christians*, as there is only one Jesus Christ and thus only one body of Christ,

❑ *World mission*, that is the task to proclaim the gospel of Jesus Christ jointly to the whole world,

❑ *Religious freedom for all religions and beliefs*, which is the other side of the coin of peaceful mission without any coercion, and

❑ *Human rights*, e.g. fighting slavery and racism.

I am convinced that both the WCC and the WEA are returning to their core history more than ever and thus find more in common than they had 30 years ago. A joint study of the early goals of our fathers and mothers in Christ helps to overcome recent struggles.

Gerhard Lindemann, not an evangelical himself, wrote a new, well researched German dissertation ('Habilitation')[2] on the early decades of the Evangelical Alliance (EA), which sheds much new light on the core topics of the WEA and shows that the WEA is much closer to its early history today than some evangelical critics to the right of WEA, suppose when they criticize the present course of WEA as being too "worldly" and too open to others.

Lindemann sees the Alliance as being, from the outset, the first organized form of ecumenism, as the sole true ecumenical organization, which emerged from revivals in the 19th century.[3] He shows that the Alliance itself frequently used the word 'ecumenical' in its early documents.[4] He writes: "It produced a climate which facilitated the founding of organizations which were the precursor of the World Council of Churches (WCC)."[5] He criticizes the fact that historical depictions of modern

---

[2] Gerhard Lindemann. Die Geschichte der Evangelischen Allianz im Zeitalter des Liberalismus (1846-1879). Theologie: Forschung und Wissenschaft, Bd. 24 [English title translation: The History of the Evangelical Alliance in the Age of Liberalism (1846-1879). Theology: Research and Scholarship, Vol. 24]. Lit Verlag: Münster, 2011.

[3] Ibid. p. 15.

[4] Ibid. p. 938, and often.

[5] Ibid. p. 945.

ecumenism often begin very late and pass over the Alliance as well as a number of its earlier leading representatives as forerunners of the unity of Christians.[6]

Lindemann sees the Alliance as a part of the transnational pietist movement of revival after Pietism,[7] which should not be judged sweepingly as 'anti-Enlightenment' or 'anti-modern'.[8] Rather, with respect to questions of religious freedom or the fight against slavery,[9] it was also ahead of its time. Fed by revival in completely different languages and cultural circles, it, like Pietism, was marked "by a wide-ranging network of international contacts and ties".[10]

The EA was founded in 1846 and was amazingly international already by 1880, but the relationship between Europe and America remained difficult and created a mildly confusing history of "Stop and Goes", until in 1951 when the present legal form was conceived under the name World Evangelical Fellowship. But Lindemann is correct when he writes about the EA of the 19th century: "Nevertheless, the body of thought of the Alliance lives on in ecumenism".[11]

After the initial success of the Ecumenical Movement in the late 19th and early 20th centuries, including the Edinburgh Missionary Conference of 1910, church leaders agreed in 1937 to establish a World Council of Churches, based on a merger of the Faith and Order Movement and Life and Work Movement organizations. The merger took place in 1938, but due to the war the WCC was founded ten years later in 1948. In 1961 the International Mission Council was added to the WCC, and in 1971, as a fourth branch, the World Council for Christian Education was added, which actually is the oldest branch, as the Sunday School Movement already started in the 18th century.

The WCC itself was thus founded in the beginning stage of the Cold War in 1948, as was the present legal form of WEA in 1951. I think that post-war developments influenced both for the better and for worse, much more than the actors have usually seen, especially as theological topics seemed to be at the top of the agendas, while often it was actually politics and social changes that made the difference.

Changes after 1989 and 2001

The WCC and the WEA both live in the same surrounding world, which left its marks on both decade by decade. I think that two dates of world history have changed the WCC and the WEA more than any other dates and developments. Events of world history very much influenced their relationship to a larger extent for the worse some decades ago and to a larger extent for the better in the last two decades.

The **first** was the end of the cold war with the breakdown of the Soviet empire 1989/90, which ended the need for countries (and even churches) to take sides with one of the super powers or to try to stay "neutral".

---

[6] Ibid. p. 21.

[7] Ibid. p. 25.

[8] Ibid. p. 25.

[9] Ibid. p. 28-29.

[10] Ibid. p. 33.

[11] Ibid. p. 946.

The **second** was the act of terror against the World Trade Centre in Manhattan on September 11, 2001 symbolizing the rise of violent branches of world religions and the rising need to speak up for peace within and between religions and also for religious freedom.

Before I elaborate on some of the consequences, let me say one thing: Our task today is neither to fight or win nor to just say nice words to each other, but as Christian leaders to understand new horizons in Christianity's history by looking back into history and learning from it, so that we can develop a better future. So let me openly give my personal evaluation of the recent decades. I do not want to offend anyone in the WCC or the WEA but to stimulate positive discussion. I hope to be fair by being self-critical and by pointing at obstacles on both sides, not just painting a black picture on one side, and a white one on the other.

The consequences of the end of the cold war are especially of interest for our host nation, **Korea**, as the situation of the cold war is still present here due to the division of the country, which may make it more difficult for Koreans to understand why the development has gone so differently in other parts of the world. Having grown up in a divided Germany and knowing how this division overshadowed everyday life, politics, and church life, even family life, as often families were split between East and West-Germany – as they are between North and South Korea – I can easily grasp the situation. With regard to my country I am glad the division is over, which was partly due to committed Christians praying and acting. I have made it my personal prayer that North Korea gets freedom and religious freedom as soon as possible. When WEA representatives under the leadership of our Secretary General Geoff Tunnicliffe visited the DMZ (Demilitarized Zone between South and North Korea) last year, it also was our common prayer and desire.

WCC Changes after 1989

Relation to Communism/Socialism

Historians have already written extensively on the changes within world Christianity because of the end of the cold war. This includes research into the changes within the WCC after 1990.[12] Similar research into the changes of the WEA is missing but would be vital.

During the cold war, the WCC leaned more toward the Socialist camp, especially concerning the future of countries in Africa, the Middle East and Asia. The WEA leaned more towards the Capitalistic camp, especially as the US influence on its leadership was still quite large. Even though this is, of course, a very rough and generalizing description, after 1990 the debates of the Cold War gradually faded away. The Majority World countries and cultures were not merely the 'Third World' anymore, but could choose their way independently along the two cold war poles, and the pluralism in political views of the member churches of both WCC and WEA grew significantly. The sometimes open, sometimes subtle accusations of pro-com-

---

[12] Eg. Klaus Koschorke (ed.). Falling Walls – the Year 1989/90 as a Turning Point in the History of World Christianity. Wiesbaden: Harrassowitz Verlag, 2009.

munism or anti-communism, even though rarely to be found in official statements, and rarely found true when taking a closer look, no longer play a role.[13]

In the 1970's there was a lot of criticism of programs within the anti-racism program of WCC, financially helping militant movements in Africa like ANC, SWAPO or Zimbabwe African National Union, where weapons might have been bought. The WEA, on the other side, was often weak in combating racism. Today, the WCC and the WEA have both left parts of their history behind and can unite in a fight against racism, but with peaceful means.

Persecution of Christians and Religious Freedom

One topic that, in my opinion, fell prey to the cold war was religious freedom. The WCC was very hesitant and had no place for persecuted pastors like Richard Wurmbrandt, founder of Voice of the Martyrs/Hilfsaktion Märtyrerkirche, who reported from the cruel communist prisons in Romania, often simply not believing these reports. In some cases there followed an official apology after 1990.

At the same time, evangelicals need to be criticized for having concentrated too much on the communist world when speaking about the persecution of Christians. The broad persecution and discrimination of Christians in Muslim countries or in countries like Sri Lanka or Nepal only became a major global topic after 1990. That seemed to prove to critics that the claim of persecution followed political interests. And before 1990, speaking up for religious freedom seemed to be just in favour of Christians; the others always seemed to be the enemy.

Nowadays, especially since 9/11, we have a clearer global picture which religious and non-religious states and movements suppress Christian churches and that other religions do not only consist of offenders, but also of a much larger number of victims.

I am glad that the WCC speaks up in favour of religious freedom and persecuted Christians much more often and more clearly than it did 30 years ago. I am also glad that the WEA has revived its historical stance for religious freedom of *all* religious and non-religious people. How both come together could be seen in the international symposium on the abuse of blasphemy law in Pakistan in Geneva at the headquarter of the WCC and at a side hearing at the UN-Human Rights Council in which we participated with a high ranking WEA delegation.

I have to add that the common experience of discrimination, persecution and suffering often has brought Christians and churches closer together in prayer, faith and action. This is not an automatic development. Historically there have been serious splits between churches under persecution. But shared suffering can also bring Christians together, who otherwise were conveniently living without relating to each other. I believe that this unity in suffering and even in martyrdom has its own – sometimes better known, sometimes even hidden – part in bringing Christians together.

---

[13] The fact that the split also had to do with the influence of more liberal theology in Europe and more conservative theology in America will be mentioned below under 'Christianity moves south to the Majority World'.

Orthodox Churches

Also following 1989, the large Russian Orthodox Church and the smaller Orthodox member churches of the WCC (including the Old-Oriental Churches like the Syrian, Armenian and Coptic Church) from the former communist countries gained a new role in their countries. They no longer had to grapple with communist governments, became more conservative at large, laid much more emphasis on theology than on politics, contrary to what they had done before, and even started to question their role within the WCC for some time.

The new self-confidence of the Orthodox churches brought them closer to the WEA in several ethical questions, enabled dialogue between their theologians and evangelical theologians, but also made the differences between certain Orthodox and evangelical views and methods more obvious. Where Orthodox churches are discriminated minorities, they profit significantly from the evangelical fight for their religious freedom, even though in Orthodox majority countries Evangelicals often are in a difficult position.

I have to add that Evangelicals only recently followed other Western churches in no longer denying orthodoxy to the Old-Oriental Churches that are older than the West-East division of 1054, especially the Syrian, Armenian and Coptic Church. Like the Catholic Church, most evangelical systematic theologians see their Christology now as being the same in content, even though using different definitions of terms.

Excursus: Evangelicals and Historic Churches

Let me add some sociological remarks here:

1. Evangelical groups overall have the highest percentage of Christians who come from a non-Christian background and become Christians as adults or at least as teenagers. Only among sects like the Mormons or Jehovah's Witnesses are there sometimes higher percentages of first generation adherents. The evangelical movement is rapidly growing among non-Christians in Africa and Asia (primarily through the witness of Africans and Asians), with the result of many new Christians with no local or general history of peaceful interaction of an established church within a culture. In Turkey, for example, 95% of all evangelicals are converts from Islam. Of course, they draw much more attention and threats than the historic churches, which often have paid for their existence the price of never engaging with the rest of the population.

2. Evangelical groups seldom represent old autochthon churches. There are no 'Evangelical' countries like there are Catholic, Orthodox, Anglican, or Lutheran countries. Even though they make up hundreds of millions, Evangelicals are not the major religious grouping in any country of the world, with the possible exception of Guatemala.

3. Many evangelical groups have large branches within traditional and main line churches, often going back to revival movements within those churches. These evangelical members tend to be very active church members and stir up much more discussion in the denominations, hopefully often for the better, but sometimes also for the worse.

Reconciled Diversity

That a major shift in its self-understanding took place within the WCC after 1989 has been stated by the WCC itself. Konrad Raiser, WCC General Secretary 1992 to 2004, spoke about a crisis and named it 'Ecumenism in Transition', calling for a major paradigm shift.[14] Even though long retired, Konrad Raiser is still calling for a stronger dialogue with Pentecostals and Evangelicals in the Global South year after year, and repeated his call just some weeks ago.

The Danish Lutheran Viggo Mortensen, having worked in leadership positions of the Lutheran World Federation, describes the profound changes within the ecumenical movement and the WCC after 1989,[15] especially, to use his words, as "Many in the ecumenical movement had … harboured the socialist dream",[16] a dream that died after 1990.[17] The development, he says, went from an emphasis on the visible and stated unity and a consensus – even when paying a high price for it – to a more visible profile and confession, and an emphasis on a reconciled diverse picture of churches and positions.

Let me give the paradigm shift two names from two prominent slogans of WCC: From "Growth in Agreement"[18] to "Reconciled Diversity". Even though this is more a shift in emphasis, and the latter concept always has been one of several propagated by the Lutheran World Federation, it helped to improve the relationship with the WEA. Accepting the diversity also made it easier to understand Evangelicals and Pentecostals in their otherness.

On the other side, during the same time span, the WEA became much more aware of the broad spectrum of theologies and confessions among its members. The growth of the Pentecostal movement also led to valuable discussions about what really constitutes the essence of evangelicalism and of the Christian faith. This promoted the understanding that it is *the kaleidoscope of evangelicalism* that is as much its strength – from its inception – as is the concentration on the central message that gave the movement its name, the 'evangel', the gospel. As an evangelical, I believe that Jesus died and rose for my salvation, and this is the centre of my and our faith; it is that which marks us as "evangelical".

Christianity Moves South to the Majority World

It is my conviction that in the time of the cold war both the WCC and the WEA had a very Western outlook and agenda. The WCC was more dominated by a European Western perspective, the WEA more by a North American one, but not only did the funds and most of the staff come from Western churches, but it was Western theologians and Western theologies that were the bench marks. In the WCC more Europe-

---

[14] Konrad Raiser. Ecumenism in Transition: A Paradigm Shift in the Ecumenical Movement? Geneva: WCC Publications, 1994.

[15] Viggo Mortensen. "From Visible Unity to Reconciled Diversity". pp. 429-441 in: Koschorke. Falling Walls.

[16] Ibid. p. 439.

[17] Ibid. p. 439.

[18] Harding Meyer et al (ed.). Growth in Agreement. Geneva: WCC Publications, 1984. Two other volumes were published in 2000 and 2007.

an liberal theology was observed, whereas in the WEA more American or Anglo-Saxon conservative theology was found. Churches in the Global South were a 'Third World'- even in theology - and had to decide for themselves between the two, even though I know that this is a very short and generalized description.[19]

Nobody has given a more condensed yet well-researched record of how Christianity wandered south and moved its centre to the Majority World (or 'Two-Thirds World', or 'Global South'), than Philip Jenkins in his book 'The Next Christendom: The Coming of Global Christianity', especially in his second edition.[20] What is most important is his summary: "Global South Christians retain a very strong supernatural orientation and are by and large far more interested in personal salvation than in radical politics."[21] He is not only speaking here about Evangelicals and about the fact that charismatic and Pentecostal revivals touched many historic mainline churches in Latin America, Africa and Asia, but more precisely about the fact that a materialistic philosophy never had much influence on theology and faith in the Global South, contrary to the influence materialistic philosophy had in the West.

Asia has become one of the big centres of Christianity and is the leading continent in absolute numbers. South Korea is second only in number of missionaries in all the world to the USA – be it Catholic, Protestant, Evangelical or Pentecostal missionaries, and India and China have each more domestic fulltime and lay evangelists from all Christian branches than any other country. And if the vastly growing number of Catholics, evangelicals, and others eager to evangelize China and the whole world get political freedom to do so, this development will rapidly speed up.

But this development is especially true for Evangelicals and the WEA. While in 1960 still *two thirds* of Evangelicals lived in the West (Europe, North America, Pacific), today it is only around *22%*, meaning the percentage has shrunk to one fourth.[22] The fast growth of Evangelicalism, often also in mainline churches like the Anglican Churches in Africa, not only assured that Western Evangelicals are now a minority, but also that the churches in the Global South started to speak with each other on the same level, not as the Big and the Small.

This becomes evident, when you look at the figures for 2011 regarding what percentage of Christianity (including Catholics) is evangelical in large regions of the world:

39% of Christianity in Asia is evangelical, with approximately 35% and 36% in Africa and North America. In the Pacific World, it is a little less than 25%, which equals the worldwide average. In Latin America and the Caribbean, it is 17% and 16%, in Europe only 3%.[23]

---

[19] Of course, there was an influential equivalent to European liberal theology in America and Evangelicals in Europe brought American theological training and positions to Europe, but in the overall this only backs what I want to say.

[20] Philip Jenkins. The Next Christendom: The Coming of Global Christianity. Oxford: Oxford University Press, 2007².

[21] Ibid. p. 8.

[22] Operation World. Colorado Springs: Biblica, 2010². p. 3.

[23] Ibid. p. 914. – This also shows, that European Christianity has only a small evangelical presence, while in America, and now even more so in Asia and Africa, the evangelical presence is very strong,

If it were not for finances, both the WCC and the WEA would be totally dominated by Southern Christians today. And if Western publishing houses did not continue to dominate global theological book production, theology would be Southern theology in the main.[24] Let me give just one example from the area of my own expertise. Western theology more or less still refuses to accept martyrdom, persecution, suffering, discrimination of Christians as vital part of Systematic Theology, Ethics, Church History or Practical Theology, as it has rarely been their problem.[25] However, for many churches in the Global South, suffering is part of their experience, identity, and theology![26]

One further word concerning the growth of the Evangelical world: the WCC and the WEA are now about the same size when it comes to the combined number of all churches involved; this makes it somehow easier to talk to each other and be equal to each other than decades ago. World Christianity today – with the exception of groups not collaborating with other Christians at all – can be roughly divided into *one half Catholic, one fourth WCC, and one fourth WEA.*

Many splits have been exported from Western Christianity to the Global South. But let's not become one-sided here: there are also genuine splits between churches in the Global South or the Majority world which originated locally. However, on a whole, Christians in many countries in the Majority World are no longer willing to copy Western splits and discussions but cooperate along other lines than a WCC and WEA divide. At the same time it is not only the larger number of churches in the Majority World, but also the fact that they are becoming increasingly independent of 'Western' funds, both in the WCC and the WEA, and thus they are more free to state their case.

Pentecostals

Much of the increased convergence in unity and mission between the WCC and the WEA is the result of the charismatic movement and the Pentecostal churches, especially as they emphasize life and experience more than following certain theologians or theologies. Many personal bonds grew here beyond any church politics.

Evangelicals recently are very much driven by the enthusiasm of the Majority World, no longer by the Western type of religion. And there is a rising merger between the Pentecostal movements and Evangelicalism.

In a very generalizing description one could say that Evangelical liturgy and spirituality is becoming more charismatic and Pentecostal, while Pentecostal theology is becoming more evangelical in its soteriology and ecclesiology. Today by and large the Pentecostal movement is an integral part of the Evangelical movement and of the

---

which also brings Evangelicals from Asia and Africa into the membership of WCC.

[24] See Soong-Chan Rah. The Next Evangelicalism: Freeing the Church from the Western Cultural Captivity. IVP: Downers Grove (IL), 2009. Still most of the Southern theologians publish in Western publishing houses and journals – mainly for academic reputation.

[25] A lot of good studies were produced in Germany after National Socialism, but were speedily forgotten after 1950.

[26] Christof Sauer, Richard Howell (ed.). Suffering, Persecution and Martyrdom: Theological Reflections. AcadSA, Johannesburg & Bonn: VKW 2011.

WEA. Within the top leadership positions of WEA, it is hard to distinguish between them. Yet, many Pentecostal leaders have taken the freedom to have a close relationship to leaders outside the WEA camp and within the ecumenical structures in their countries and regions.

Excursus: Evangelicals outside WEA

I would like to add two remarks concerning Evangelicals outside the WEA.

1. There are Evangelicals – very much depending on the definition of 'evangelical' – that do not cooperate with the national evangelical alliances and see working together with other denominations and Christian confessions as evil in itself. My well-informed estimate would be that they make up 100 million beyond the 600 million within the WEA.

As the WCC does not feel responsible for whatever Protestants or Orthodox people anywhere in the world do or say, so the WEA should not be taken hostage to what any supposed Evangelical somewhere in the world says or does, and surely not those who clearly distance themselves from any alliance of evangelicals. The WEA stands for what it officially is, says and does, as does the WCC or any other global body.

2. One of the lowest percentages of Evangelicals organized within a national alliance is to be found in the USA. In the USA, there are more Evangelicals outside the WEA than inside. To compare this with Germany: Probably more than 95% of the Evangelicals are represented by the national alliance. The large Southern Baptist Convention in the US does not belong to the WEA, and most tele-evangelists in the USA do not like the cooperation within the National Association of Evangelicals (NAE) or WEA.

Thus whatever happens among evangelicals or right wing Christians in the USA does not always reflect what the NAE stands for and surely not what the international evangelical community represented by the WEA stands for. The WEA is shocked when tele-evangelists call for all non-Christians to leave the USA or if Christians on the fringe burn Qurans; the WEA has always spoken clearly against these developments.

Theology and Experts

Within the WEA the role of experts is on the rise. Even though it is part of the WEA's tradition that it is not run just by theologians and ordained clergy, the emphasis on the priesthood of all believers was in tension with the need for experts. If you want to engage in judicial religious freedom cases, fighting poverty, working on the UN level or get involved in major declarations with the Vatican and the WCC, experts are needed. I think the WEA has meanwhile found a much better way of pairing the use of experts, even world class experts, with the task of representing a global movement, not just the opinion of a few. The WEA is vision driven, but it knows that in our complex world specialized knowledge is necessary to work for the good of all in certain areas.

It is not by chance that our experts paved the way in certain joint activities of the WCC and the WEA by diligently discussing the issues at stake first in a non-public atmosphere. The role of experts makes the relationship to the WCC easier, as experts often know more about the other side, find an easier way to each other, and because of their expertise, the structures at large can then decide whether this is good for all and in line with the overall vision or not.

Notable is also the rise of Pentecostal academic theology[27] that automatically increased the average training level within world evangelicalism.

Social Engagement

The whole question of engagement for a better world, for example fighting racism, poverty, and human trafficking, often fell prey to the cold war too. While the tendency in the WCC was to question certain types of mission but to take any social engagement as a given truth, evangelicals had the tendency to concentrate on world mission and forgot about the numerous Biblical commandments to help the poor and treat all humans as equal, even though their real engagement often was much better than their words.

From my perspective, it is partly due to the cold war that a lot of social engagement came under the suspicion by many evangelicals that it was Christianized socialism.[28]

Evangelicals have always been involved in social action, even on a global level, as the fight against slavery connected with the person and name of William Wilberforce proves. One of the founders of the German Evangelical Alliance, Theodor Christlieb, Professor of Practical Theology at Bonn State University, fought for years at the International Alliance conferences against the Indo-British opium trade. Through a book translated into several languages and discussed in the British parliament, as well as through other means, he argued that it was both immoral politics and an immoral way of doing mission, and a wrong mixture of presenting the gospel by using political and military pressure.[29]

But movements like Micah Network/Micah Challenge and large organizations like World Vision have it much easier since the end of the cold war to be understood by evangelicals as just putting biblical commands into practice.

The problem of the evangelicals has never been their view of religious freedom or its history of social engagement, but that for a long time they departed from their own history by staying away from society, poverty and politics. In reality, the Evangelical Alliance is one of the oldest human rights movement or organization, even though this has fallen into oblivion among evangelicals today.

---

[27] See, for example, Wolfgang Vondey. Beyond Pentecostalism: the Crisis of Global Christianity and the Renewal of the Theological Agenda. Grand Rapids (Mi): Wm. B. Eerdmans, 2010.

[28] If I would have time, I would also comment on the strange mix of right wing religion and politics in the USA, but I have to point to what I stated above that large parts of those evangelicals are outside the US members of WEA, the National Association of Evangelicals.

[29] See my article „Christlieb, Theodor". S. 188 in: A. Scott Moreau (Hg.). Evangelical Dictionary of World Missions. Grand Rapids (MI): Baker Books & Carlisle (GB): Paternoster Press , 2000 and my first doctoral thesis: Theodor Christlieb und seine Missionstheologie. Wuppertal: Telos, 1985.

Human Rights

It is no doubt that even the fight for human rights often was overshadowed by the cold war. Western countries felt morally superior by proving what was wrong in communist countries – making it quite difficult to speak about problems in their own Western countries. Communist countries countered by arguing that capitalism in itself is directed against human rights.

It took two decades from the inception of the Universal Declaration of Human Rights, which was not legally binding, to the three major legally binding covenants of 1966/1976 and again to the three large UN conventions on racial discrimination, protection of children and protection of migrant workers 1984-1990.[30] Since 1990, human rights questions are no longer connected to the East-West-conflict, and even in the debate over human rights with China or Muslim states, the arguments no longer arise from the cold war; now the problematic claim is that human rights are not universal but have to be culturally developed.

The WCC emerged at the same time as the UN, and when the Universal Declaration was written, WCC people even played a major role in developing the human rights canon. The WCC was in favour of this from its inception, much earlier than many of its member churches.

The evangelical movement got its name during the fight against slavery, and it probably was here that for the first time the unity between Christians in a state church and all minor 'free' churches was practiced. And in the 19th century it was as much a human rights movement as a mission movement towards Christian unity.

It is a pity that the WCC and the WEA rarely, if ever, worked together in the fight against human rights violations during the cold war. And it is a huge relief that beyond our ongoing discussions on the Bible, on mission and on a theology of non-Christian religions, the world can now see that the WCC and the WEA (as well as the Vatican) are major champions of human rights on all levels, each for itself and all together. We also can learn now from more individualistic approaches to human rights and from more community oriented approaches, as both are backed by biblical and Christian principles. Fighting racism is as much a personal human right as it is a program for law and society.

Changes after 9/11: The Relation to Other Religions

At least since the Second Vatican Council claimed to see God at work in all other religions and exchanged the view of religions being rival and wrong ways to God for a positive view of other religions, the relationship between Christianity and other religions became dominant in Christian theological debate. The key and often only question for quite some time was whether people can be saved outside the Christian faith. In simplified form, this boiled down to a debate between stopping to do missions, on the one hand, and mission being the only relation to people of other faiths on the other hand.

---

[30] See Thomas Schirrmacher. Menschenrechte. Holzgerlingen: SCM Hänssler, 2012. An English edition is in preparation. It was not by accident that the first book in the WEA Global Issue book series was *Human Rights: A Christian Primer*, by Thomas K. Johnson. Bonn: VKW, 2008.

It is mainly due to developments symbolized by 9/11 that a whole new spectrum of questions around the relation between Christianity and other religions has come to the top of the agenda: religious freedom, differentiating between religions and their effects on society, differentiating between different wings within religions (e.g., peaceful Islam in Indonesia vs. Islamism), the difference of a dialogue of life with your neighbours and between top level religious leaders, and the question of working together for the common good, such as human rights, overcoming poverty, or peace within a country and between countries.

No longer would anyone say that the Good is to be found in every form of religion, as there are devastating forms of religions. And no one would say any longer that it is forbidden to cooperate with people of other faiths, or that you are only allowed to talk to them for the purpose of preaching.

Allen D. Hertzke, professor of sociology of religion, writing about the history of the last 20 years, described how an alliance of Evangelicals, Catholics, Jews and others in the USA and worldwide made religious freedom a topic of world politics and in the media.[31]

The new code of ethics, "Christian witness in a multi-religious world",[32] describes the new unity, by covering the whole breadth of the topic concerning dialogue with other faiths:

1. *encourage* Christians to *strengthen* their own religious identity and faith while *deepening* their knowledge and understanding of different religions, and to do so also taking into account the perspectives of the adherents of those religions. Christians should avoid misrepresenting the beliefs and practices of people of different religions.

2. *cooperate* with other religious communities engaging in interreligious advocacy towards justice and the common good and, wherever possible, standing together in solidarity with people who are in situations of conflict.

3. *call* on their governments to ensure that freedom of religion is properly and comprehensively respected, recognizing that in many countries religious institutions and persons are inhibited from exercising their mission.

In the political realm, the Evangelical Alliance has been working towards religious freedom and human rights (e.g., fighting slavery) from its very inception in mid-19th century. It is said that sometimes during the cold war this fell into oblivion.

Evangelicals have always been highly dedicated to religious freedom, including the religious freedom of non-evangelical churches. When in the middle of the 19th century, pastors of state churches and independent churches in Europe started to meet across borders, thus forming the earliest ecumenical movement, religious freedom in Europe, where religion was still often compulsory, was one of their major goals. For example, in 1852 a high-ranking delegation of the Evangelical Alliance visited the Ottoman sultan on behalf of persecuted Orthodox churches, and in this tradition to-

---

[31] Allen D. Hertzke, Freeing God's Children. The Unlikely Alliance for Global Human Rights. New York: Rowman & Littlefield, 2004.

[32] See: http://www.worldevangelicals.org/resources/source.htm?id=288 (21.11.2014).

day well equipped evangelical religious freedom lawyers have run and won cases in the European Court for Human Rights for several non-protestant churches, like the Bessarabian Church or the Greek Orthodox Church. The orthodox churches in Turkey, as well as the dying old churches in Iraq today, find their greatest help in evangelical organizations, as evangelicals heavily use international media, but also – as in the case of Germany – the help of parliament and governments.

Consistent with this longstanding intent, the 12th General Assembly of the WEA in Pattaya, Thailand (2008) voted without a dissenting vote for the "Resolution on Religious Freedom and Solidarity with the Persecuted Church".[33] In it the WEA stands for religious freedom for all religions and also clearly states that it is our task to work together with people of other or no faith towards the common good and peace in society. Paragraph 5 says:

> The WEA therefore aims to work collaboratively with all who share its goals of supporting religious freedom, be it political powers or representatives of other or no religions. The WEA affirms the intention of Christians to live together peacefully with adherents of other or no religions and to work together for the common good and reconciliation.

But then the WEA adds paragraph 6:

> The WEA differentiates between advocating the rights of members of other or no religions and endorsing the truth of their beliefs. Advocating the freedom of others can be done without accepting the truth of what they believe.

WEA initiatives, like the Peacebuilding Initiative Micah – fighting against poverty, or the International Institute for Religious Freedom – lead us to a lot of cooperation with people of other religions in the political realm.

I once met a mufti of a major Muslim country. He invited me to become a Muslim and gave me a Quran. I invited him to believe in Jesus and gave him a New Testament. Then I listened to his complaints and presented what we researched about the persecution of Christians in his country. We discussed how we could work towards more peace and less violence in his country. This is how evangelicals combine mission, dialogue, and working for peace and the common good. This perhaps is still a bit different from how the WCC does dialogue, but there is nothing standing in the way of a convergence in mission and dialogue.

Excursus
Christianity Discards Its Constantinian Shape:
Improvements in Recent Christian History

Changing one's religion – and the political unrest following it – is not a new phenomenon, but a very historic one, be it famous people like Augustine, be it whole continents (e.g., Southeast Asia to Buddhism, Europe to Christianity or Northern Africa and the Near East to Islam) and it has often played a central role in local and world politics.

---

[33] „Resolution on Religious Freedom". International Journal for Religious Freedom 2 (2009) 1: 92-94; see also http://www.iirf.eu/index.php?id=17.

Not changing one's religion in Christian, Muslim, Hindu, and Buddhist societies was very often more due to the pressure of culture and surroundings than due to conviction. In history, probably more people were forced to change their religion or to stay in their own religion, than there were people who freely and knowledgably chose or kept their religion.

In most of the past centuries, Christians, like most Muslims today, demanded that other people leave their religion and convert, but Christians, like Muslims today, did not allow people to convert from their religion. Within Christendom apostasy was sometimes punished with civil consequences, including loss of property, family, civil rights, jobs, or even one's life, as is still the case within some Muslim dominated countries.

We are experiencing the long stretched end of the Constantinian era, which includes the end of safeguarding Christianity by means of the Caesar and forcing people into the church by political, juridical, economical and other civil pressures. Most Christians feel this is not a catastrophe but an advantage. The Christian faith can again live by spiritual means and through the power of the Holy Spirit working with the Word, and does not need the help of the worldly powers, be it armies, governments or business. I believe that this does not weaken the church but that it strengthens its specific task.

Looking at the broad picture, Christianity and its churches as a whole have taken the right course in the last hundred years, abstaining more and more from violence, from being involved in wars or civil wars, and from using political means or economical pressure for missions. Even though there are still situations like in Northern Ireland or the so-called Christian terrorist organization 'National Liberation Front' (NLFT) in Northeast India or the Nagaland rebels, they occur on the extreme fringe of Christianity, and the churches or Christians involved, are criticized by the vast majority of Christians and churches worldwide. This is in sharp contrast to what happened during World War I in Europe, where many major churches fuelled the war and gave their consent to European countries getting involved in war also transferring the conflict to the whole colonial world. Thanks to God, there no longer is a broad acceptance of violence in propagating one's own message in the Christian world. There is just the opposite development as in Islam, where the Islamist acceptance of violence to conquer the world makes inroads into the Muslim community even where they lived peacefully with other groups for centuries.

The forced conversion of the Saxons by the German emperor or the Goa inquisition in India are mainly history and we Christians are glad, because they belong to the darkest pages of church history. Today millions become Christians every day, people who do not come from a Christian background, but do so by pure conviction without any pressure. More people are converting to Christianity than at any time when Christians allowed violent expansion to corrupt its message. What the gun boats of Western colonial powers did not achieve in China, the gospel message achieves today without any outside help whatsoever.

Nowadays it is more the Christian community that suffers hard persecution in certain countries and areas and the number of martyrs is growing daily. Virtually all "Christian" or former Christian countries grant religious freedom to all religions, while the number of "non-Christian countries" that do not grant the same rights to Christian churches is still high.

Our Relationship Today

❏ Concerning the relationship between WEA and the WCC, we must first mention that there is a wide spectrum of relations between WEA and the whole spectrum of WCC's member churches, reaching from the Russian Orthodox Church to evangelical or Pentecostal member churches of WCC, some of which are members of the WCC and the WEA at the same time. This is true the other way round, too. WCC has a different relationship to a wide range of national alliances according to the local situation, and to the wide range of their member churches. Thus, we need to distinguish between the relationship between the two organized bodies and the relationship of both bodies to the large spectrum of churches which the other body represents.

❏ The WEA and its members have no problem with signing the charter of the WCC, which all WCC member churches have to sign, and WCC member churches can agree with everything the confession of WEA says (even so some would miss some topics here).

❏ The WCC has more former 'state churches' as member churches, but this is changing; some former state or majority churches have recently become more conservative or even evangelical, such as large parts of the Anglican Church in Africa. On the other side, small and new churches have become more 'liberal' – forgive this short and easily misunderstood description due to the time restriction. Therefore, nowadays it is no longer possible to simply connect 'liberalism' to older and larger mainline churches, and 'conservatism' to younger, smaller and independent churches.

❏ The WEA has a larger common ground that all members share than does the WCC, even though one should not underestimate the wide range of opinions among evangelicals hiding behind the strong identity markers, like faithfulness to the Bible and evangelism, as individualism leaves its marks. In addition, the WEA has more space for individuals and volunteers without an official church office than does the WCC.

❏ The Global Christian Forum, in which WCC and WEA are involved together with the Secretaries of Christian World Communions and other bodies, is a great way to strengthen relationships between Christians globally.

One reason is that even though most people attending are sent by their church or body, nevertheless there is a strong emphasis of sharing personal experiences and faith stories. This personal element and a lot of time to get to know other delegates help a lot to overcome prejudice.

The other reason is that the global bodies engaged here, including WCC and WEA, prove with the Global Christian Forum, that their goal is not just to grow their own organization and compete with others, but first of all to grow the body of Christ and bring Christians together and provide a platform for those, who so far did not cooperate with any of the global bodies. This is why WEA sees the Global Christian Forum as a vital and important effort where it gladly invests energy.

The Future Agenda: The Bible

One topic, which from my point of view has not really been touched in the discussions between WCC and WEA and its members since the end of the cold war, is the authority of the Bible. Knowing that there is a wide range of evangelical positions concerning details, and knowing that the WCC represents a wide spectrum including Orthodox or Pentecostal churches and positions, somehow – from my point of view – Biblical authority and the conservative-liberal discussions has not yet undergone similar changes as other areas.

I am of the opinion that nothing helps more in understanding each other in our differences and in trying to find ways to more unity, than talking together in person and studying the original statements and writings of the others. I am amazed at how often theologians today still do not know people and writings from other or even opposing wings of Christianity. That is especially true in the area of Biblical scholarship. Often, if one reads theological literature, people still only quote their own – often small – camp and do not even seem to know about the existence of libraries of good works of others.

Evangelicals have learned and done a lot to favour hermeneutics and accept that – even among them – the question, how to interpret the Bible is not an easy one. And they have learned a lot from research and interpretation outside their camp. Still many have the impression that there is a deep gulf between two ways of dealing with the Bible.

The big step forward in the discussion of the 'Bible-question', and finding a common ground here, is still part of future deliberations. This unsolved problem has major consequences in the area of theological education, which often is more separated into two camps than the churches themselves. I am sorry that I cannot elaborate on this topic now, but it should be high on our agenda, especially as any convergence of WCC and WEA in mission cannot leave out academic missiology, the training of missionaries and a contextualized missional theology.

What gives me confidence here is the fact, that the Bible plays a much different, larger and broader role in everyday life of believers and churches in the Global South than in the West, as Philipp Jenkins has described so ably in his book.[34]

The WEA, its Secretary General and its Theological Commission would like to initiate a worldwide resurgence of Bible reading on grass roots level among pastors and among us all. Since more Bibles are distributed by all three major Christian global bodies (and their members) than any time before, it is strikingly odd that at the same time we have more biblically illiterate Christians than ever, not only among nominal or secularized Christians, but even at the heart of Evangelical revivals. I hope that a new Bible movement will also bring the WCC and the WEA and all Christians closer to each other when we together study the book that alone witnesses the gospel of Jesus Christ, our Saviour.

---

[34] Jenkins. Christendom. pp. 257ff: "The Bible in the South".

Appendix 1
One Lord, One Voice, One Body: Thoughts on Ephesians 4:1-6

From my devotional for the General Assembly of the World Evangelical Alliance in Pattaya in October 2008

> ... I urge you to live a life worthy of the calling ... Be completely humble and gentle; be patient, bearing with one another in love. Make every effort to keep the unity of the Spirit through the bond of peace. There is one body and one Spirit – just as you were called to one hope when you were called – one Lord, one faith, one baptism; one God and Father of all, who is over all and through all and in all. (Eph 4:1-6, NIV).

There are wrong ways to create unity among Christians. Finding the least common denominator is one of them. Here the gospel tends to become smaller and smaller with every new player involved. Selling the truth or handing over leadership to those who seem nicest is another wrong way.

However, no necessary warning of wrong ways to achieve Christian unity can nullify our task to strive for the unity of the body of Christ and to proclaim *One Lord, One Voice, One Body*. Living in unity means "to live a life worthy of our calling." Three times Paul mentions our "calling" as Christians in these verses as ground for the demand to unity. Being a Christian means to be humble, gentle, and patient to everyone especially to other Christians. Thinking about wrong ways to unity must not keep us from finding right ways to seek unity; above all, we are to "make every effort to keep the unity of the Spirit through the bond of peace".

Does this mean that we should forget about truth? No! If there is only "one God" ('theos'), then in the end there can only be one truth about God ('theology'). If there is only "one Spirit" and if it is the task of the Spirit to lead us into all truth, the Spirit and his truth will not divide but unite us. And if there is only "one faith", we never have to choose between unity and faith, but deeper and clearer faith will always lead to unity, and greater real unity will lead to a deeper and common faith.

In Ephesians 1-3 Paul uses in-depth teaching to prepare for Ephesians 4. He reveals to us who God is and who Jesus is; he explains forgiveness, resurrection, ascension, and other central topics of Christian teaching. One needs to read these chapters over and over again to understand the whole depth of their message. Paul paints a magnificent picture of God's universal purpose with the church of Jesus Christ. It is so magnificent that it seems far away from the reality of our often so ugly local churches.

So what practical outcome does the teaching in Ephesians 1-3 have? Very easy: "Thus I admonish you ... (Eph 4:1) to live and work for unity!" Paul's admonitions in Ephesians 4 are not the end of biblical revelation and teaching but the practical result of it! "Instead, speaking the truth in love, we will in all things grow up into him who is the Head, that is, Christ" (Eph 4:15).

Let us pray that the Spirit of God keeps us from wrong ways to Christian unity, but even more so, to make truly biblical and spiritual ways to Christian unity the centre of our thinking about the one church, the one body of Jesus Christ.

Appendix 2
Fourfold Essential Poles of the Evangelical Movement

The development of the first statement of faith of the Evangelical Alliance in 1846 is stirring,[35] as the first two sentences have produced a dynamic tension of complementary principles, which we must embrace and employ:

1. The divine inspiration, authority, and sufficiency of the Holy Scriptures.

2. The right and duty of private judgment in the interpretation of the Holy Scriptures.[36]

On the one hand, you find here an unalterable and unifying provision in the sufficiency of Scripture. On the other hand, it reflects an extreme pluralism, obligating each believer to interpret the foundation for himself.

Two opposite poles mark evangelicals and one does not do them justice if one only observes or stresses one pole of those positions.

Restated, on the one hand, there is the *centrality of the Holy Scriptures* inherited from the Protestant Reformation. On the other hand, there is *individual salvation* that arises from Luther's question: "How do I find a gracious God?" It is a matter of each person having a personal relationship with God and there arising as a corrective to the centrality of the Scriptures the entitlement, even the obligation, of every Christian to study the Scriptures himself and to interpret them. The result is that such an individual stands on a level with every evangelical theologian, no matter how learned, even if it is his pastor. Thus, the evangelical world unites dogmatic constriction, thanks to the position of the Bible, with an enormous democratic breadth, because every Christian is allowed to have a say.

The **second two poles** are missions and religious freedom. From the enormous emphasis on a personal relationship with Jesus arose a strong stress on the 'duty to witness' as well as a strong emphasis on religious freedom. The concept of voluntariness marks not only free churches. Rather, it also marks intra-church pietism as faith, which should not be something that is only external, or inherited, but rather something which is personally experienced. Above all no one can be forced into it. Indeed, coercion destroys the possibility of accomplishing a truly independent, personal repentance before God. Thus, we prefer a smaller church with convinced members to a large church with many members who belong only due to societal, familial, or other pressures.

A typical example is the relationship to the Catholic Church. At the time of the founding of the Evangelical Alliance, its advocacy of freedom of religion and freedom of conscience represented the complete opposite of the Ultramontanist Catholic Church, which decidedly rejected religious freedom (and human rights) as being atheistic in favour of a Catholic State. Thus, the religious freedom approach of the Alliance met its utmost opposition in the development of the Catholic Church on its way to papal infallibility (1870). The Alliance's emphasis on the primacy of voluntary personal conversion excluded any sort of coercion in missions or religious coer-

---

[35] Lindemann. Geschichte. pp. 87-98.

[36] Ibid. p. 98.

cion from the side of a Christian state. This is pure history now, because since Vatican II and by the latest statement "Christian Witness ..." the Catholic Church has become a major proponent of religious freedom as a Christian principle.

But at the time of political tension between evangelicals and Catholics, it was the Evangelical Alliance who defended discriminated Catholics in Protestant countries. For example when the Alliance opposed Sweden with a delegation in 1858, after the highest royal court had expelled six women from the country who had converted to Catholicism, by calling for religious freedom for these Catholics, there was throughout Europe a storm of outrage outside of the Alliance.[37] The Alliance was then significantly involved in the Swedish Parliament's 1860 abolishment of the penalties for leaving the Lutheran State Church.

Appendix 3
My Personal Position on Dialogue

Dialogue is a Christian virtue when it means peaceful discussion, honest, patient listening and learning from others. A dialogue between convinced Christians and believers of other religions is possible, insofar as Christians are willing to speak peacefully about their faith with others ("always be ready to give a reason for the hope that is in you but with meekness and respect", 1Pet 3:15) "and listen to others" (Jam 1:19). They wish to learn from others' experiences in many aspects of life (see esp. the Book of Proverbs) and are willing to call themselves and their behaviour into question.

Dialogue is also an important part of working towards peace in a society, as Paul commands us: "If it is possible, as far as it depends on you, live at peace with everyone." (Rom 12:18), following Jesus' blessing: "Blessed are the peacemakers, for they will inherit the earth." (Mt 5:5)

But dialogue which surrenders Christianity's assertion of truth or abandons world missions is inconceivable, for it gives up Christianity itself. Dialogue which requires the Christian to temporarily or principally waive the claims of absolute truth about Jesus Christ (Jn 14:6), the Gospel (Rom 1:16-17, 2:16) or the Word of God (2Tim 3:16-17, Heb 4:12-13, Jn 17:17), so that Biblical revelation is equated with the beliefs of other religions or world views, cannot be reconciled with Christian missions or with the essence of Christianity itself.

Christianity's assertion of authority is above all expressed in the doctrines of the Last Judgment and of Eternal Life. Hebrews 6:1-2 describes the 'resurrection of the dead and of eternal judgment' as two of the six most important elements of our faith, and as the Apostolic Creed says, 'he will return to judge both the quick and the dead'. At the same time, it is God himself who will be the judge, and not us, and he has postponed this judgment for a long age of grace, of which we are ambassadors of love and grace, not of judgment.

As humans, we can only see the outward appearance, but God alone can see the hearts of men (1Sam 16:7). This is why he alone dispenses absolute just judgment taking into account everything that can be known about a person.

---

[37] Lindemann. Geschichte. pp. 295-300.

Appendix 4
Fundamentalism is a Militant Truth Claim

In my opinion, one should only speak of fundamentalism when violence is involved or a true danger for internal security exists.

Since the September 11, 2001 attacks, fundamentalists are understood by the public to be mostly radical, violence-prone, religiously motivated extremists or even simply religious terrorists. What is meant in common parlance with the word 'fundamentalism' is, however, *a militant truth claim*, and precisely that is what I find to be the shortest definition.

There are, in my opinion, only two possibilities for saving the term 'fundamentalism' for legitimate use. First, the term fundamentalism could be brought closer to its everyday linguistic usage and thus employed with respect to movements truly identified with violence. Alternatively, taking the direction of a broader use of the term to apply to all sorts of movements could be desirable, which then means that the term urgently has to be de-emotionalized so that it achieves a neutral, non-pejorative meaning. For this to be achieved there must be large-scale action by experts opposing the mass media's approach, which at the moment is an illusion.

In my opinion, those who warn the public about fundamentalist movements should limit themselves to those groups who are dangerous due to their basic justification for using violence. Additionally, warnings are warranted when it comes to movements demonstrating an inclination towards violence, of course also those using force, and lastly those from whom the danger is at least emanating that they might want to achieve political power over dissenters by the use of undemocratic means. For that reason my definition is as follows:

> *Fundamentalism is a militant truth claim, which derives its claim to power from non-disputable, higher revelation, people, values, or ideologies. It is aimed against religious freedom and calls for peace and justifies, urges, or uses non-state or state-based non-democratic force in order to accomplish its goals. In the process, it often invokes opposition to certain achievements of modernity in favour of historical grandeur and bygone eras, and at the same time it uses these modern achievements mostly in order to extend and produce a modern variation of older religions and world views. Fundamentalism is a transformation of a religion or worldview conditioned by modernity.*

I hold the view that a religious and worldview community, which stands for, propagates, and in practice respects the freedom of religion cannot be fundamentalist, and should not be called fundamentalist! The reverse also applies. The rejection of religious freedom is a clear indicator of a fundamentalist direction, albeit not the sole indicator.

In the same way, I also hold the position that a religious and worldview community that stands for, propagates, and in practice respects classic human rights cannot be fundamentalist and should not be called fundamentalist! However, this is not so easy to achieve, just as is the case with religious freedom. The reason is that the term human rights has more and more moved from the classic sense of human rights and has been expanded to inflated demands. If abortion is defined as a human right, then most religious communities are dealt bad cards, because they still assess the rights of the unborn to be on equal bar to those of the mother, or at least assert that the rights of the unborn should be borne in mind.

But back to religious freedom: What more can a person demand from a religious community in a 'modern' democratic state than that it advocates religious freedom so that there is a religious neutrality to the state as well as a separation of church and state, or that there is a neutral religious structure which at the same time respects other religions and worldviews?

The Heart of Church and Mission

Bryan Knell

This book brings together a passion for the church and a passion for global mission. It looks at the heart of the UK church, asking whether and how it beats for mission and explores the passion of the mission community, and asks how it involves the local church. You might be forgiven for expecting that the heart of church and the heart of mission would be interwoven and closely linked together, but that has not been the case.

Two significant historical events continue to shape the church and mission in the Western World. Christendom removed mission from the church and the launch of the missionary societies disengaged the local church from mission. Although there is plenty of talk of change, the dominant mind-set is still shaped by these events. Practical suggestions are directed at churches and agencies with the aim of re-establishing, Mission at the heart of the church and the church at the heart of mission.

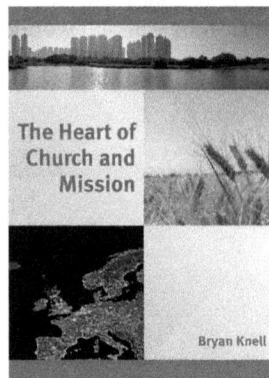

The world is a different place to when the "modern" Western mission movement developed. Yet many of the same structures exist today, in both churches and mission agencies. The church in the West needs to engage in new and appropriate ways in the world, building on history but not being bound by it. Bryan's prophetic call is to new ways of thinking, new attitudes and clear Biblical principles and deserves a wide audience. The Global Church deserves no less than a fresh approach to obeying His command to join together in God's mission in His world.

Martin Lee, Executive Director, Global Connections, UK

Pb. • pp. 80 • £ 6.00 • US$ 9.99 • € 9.95
ISBN 978-3-95776-037-1

VTR Publications • Gogolstr. 33 • 90475 Nürnberg • Germany
info@vtr-online.com • http://www.vtr-online.com

www.ingramcontent.com/pod-product-compliance
Lightning Source LLC
Chambersburg PA
CBHW071138090426
42736CB00012B/2152